Constitutional

REASON OF STATE

THE COLVER LECTURES
IN BROWN UNIVERSITY
1956

OTHER BOOKS BY CARL J. FRIEDRICH

The Age of the Baroque, 1610-1660

Constitutional Government and Democracy

Foreign Policy in the Making

Inevitable Peace

The New Belief in the Common Man

Responsible Bureaucracy
(with Taylor Cole)

Totalitarian Dictatorship and Autocracy
(with Zbigniew K. Brzezinski)

Editor of

The Philosophy of Hegel

The Philosophy of Kant

Politica Methodice Digesta of
Johannes Althusius

Studies in Federalism
(with Robert R. Bowie)

Constitutional
REASON OF STATE

The Survival of the Constitutional Order

C. J. FRIEDRICH

PROVIDENCE · RHODE ISLAND

Brown University Press
1957

PREFACE

THE PRESENT STUDY proposes to explore the history of the
problem of "reason of state" in a constitutional political order.
The writers treated belong among the "great" in modern
political thought and therefore it is not and cannot be a question of dealing with the integral thought of the writers here
examined. All we can hope to do is to seek out those aspects
which bear more immediately upon this particular problem.
Ratio status,—the very term shows that we are moving within
the context of the great tradition of Western rationalism, where
everything has its particular *ratio* or inner rationale which it
behoves the mind to grasp and to understand. For the idea of
such *rationes* is prominent in the Middle Ages,—an aspect
of the matter which receives scant attention in Friedrich
Meinecke's magistral treatment of the subject *Die Idee der
Staatsräson in der Neueren Geschichte* published in 1925 and
by now become something of a classic (see Appendix). Perhaps
partly because of his lack of sympathy for this *rational* basis
of the idea which he was discussing, he also paid scant attention to that aspect of it which we are particularly concerned
with here: reason of state in its application to the government
of law, the constitutional order, in short "constitutional reason
of state" or more precisely "reason of the constitutional state."
In light of this focus of my study, I have severely restricted

myself also in giving references to secondary works. The literature on the writers here touched upon is of course very large, and I have referred only to those who had a distinct contribution to make to what I am here discussing, or who were of recent vintage and therefore perhaps not so well known. No doubt the specialist will miss many an important item.

While my studies on the subject here presented extend over many years,—I already had occasion to deal with it in my introduction to Althusius,—a grant by the John Simon Guggenheim Memorial Foundation provided the opportunity to pull some of the material together, and I am very grateful to it for this help. Actually these studies also extend to a comparative analysis of present-day efforts in a number of countries to cope practically with the problems of security and survival in face of internal and external subversion threats. This comparative analysis which I hope to complete soon is in turn related to the treatment of "constitutional dictatorship" in my *Constitutional Government and Democracy* (ed. 1950, ch. XXVI) in its contrast with totalitarian dictatorship (about which I have recently published a comparative analysis, together with Z. Brzezinski). In turn, the security problem has presented itself in its peculiar acuteness to modern constitutional systems precisely because of the totalitarian challenge. It is generally agreed that constitutional systems are faced with their most deadly danger in this connection, and hence it is touched upon briefly, by way of providing a setting for the historical studies here presented.*
I originally intended to publish these two approaches to the problem of constitutional reason of state in one study. But an

* I should have liked to include also the somewhat marginal, but highly significant thought of Pascal, Vico and the Utopians (More, Campanella, Fénélon), but since none of these were "constitutionalists" in the strict sense, I shall hope to deal with them in another connection.

invitation to give the Colver Memorial Lectures at Brown University in the general field of political thought, to be published by them, persuaded me to prepare the material here presented as a separate treatment. As a matter of fact, I was able to present only part of this material in the lectures themselves, but I want to thank the Trustees and more especially Professor Guy Howard Dodge for their confidence. The main theme of "constitutional reason of state" has also been presented to some groups of scholars in Europe, more especially at the Universities of Turin, Strasbourg, Munich and Oxford. Thanks are due to Professors Wheare, Moushkely, Crosa and Pfister for arranging these opportunities to submit my hypotheses to critical discussion. Professor George L. Mosse was good enough to read the manuscript in its entirety and to offer some very helpful criticisms. My editorial assistant, Miss Roberta G. Hill, gave her usual invaluable aid with manuscript, proofs and index. Other indebtedness I have tried to acknowledge in the footnotes.

Table of Contents

Introduction

Some Thoughts on Security and Survival

CHRISTOPHER MARLOWE, IN HIS PLAY *The Jew of Malta,* presents Machiavelli in a prologue which echoes the shock that Christian thinkers had felt, when confronted with Machiavelli's demand that all claims of personal ethics and morality be subordinated to the requirements of the security and survival of the republic.

> Though some speak openly against my books,
> Yet will they read me, and thereby attain
> To Peter's chair; and when they cast me off,
> Are poison'd by my climbing followers.
>
> . . .
> What right had Caesar to his crown?

Clearly, Machiavelli is here made to stand for an unprincipled belief in personal success of men who ruthlessly climb the ladder to power, including "St. Peter's chair." Such a doctrine is a far cry from Machiavelli's real concern, namely the concern for the state which for him, as for the ancients the *polis,* the *civitas,* was the essential prerequisite of all virtue. Only within the political community can men achieve true nobility. Therefore the building and maintaining of the political community becomes a task of primary value. The accomplishment is the condition of all moral conduct and hence cannot in turn be made to depend upon the laws which govern this conduct. An inexorable logic which sounds familiar enough at the present time.

But why revive the ancient verbiage? Why talk about "reason of state," when actually a term such as "constitutional defense" provides so much more convenient an expression? Because, as I hope to show, the concept of the reason of state helps to face the hard core of the issue which such terms as "constitutional defense" and "national interest" tend to obscure. Furthermore, it is in terms of reason of state that the issue has been debated in the past, and some light may be shed upon our present difficulties by the hard-headed reflections of pre-liberal political thought.

In doing this, we have to admit, however, that internal and external security get hopelessly mixed up with each other. This was, as we shall see, the inclination of all the older writers, usually without any explicit recognition of the fact.

This tendency is strikingly illustrated by Montesquieu's transformation of Locke's federative power into the executive power of his own doctrine. He accomplishes it by pointing out that dealing with foreign relations, the "design of foreigners" of Locke, involves the problem of insurrection and the like. For they are often fomented by foreign powers, and furthermore he who seeks to overthrow the government puts himself in the position of a foreign enemy.[1] It is therefore perhaps better to *accept* the difficulties resulting from this intermingling of external and internal security, as far as the broad theoretical discussion is concerned, than to attempt a separation, which would be artificial at best.

[1] See Book XI, chapter VI, of *Esprit des Lois,* as well as the discussion in my "Pouvoir dans la Théorie Constitutionaliste" in *Pouvoir—Annales de l'Institut International de la Philosophie Politique* (1956), and the references given there.

2

In a sense, what we are dealing with here is the broad issue of "politics and morals." But we are proposing to approach it in terms essentially political rather than moral.[2]

It used to be considered axiomatic that human beings had, by the law of nature, the right to defend themselves. But this proposition was formal, in the sense that it left open the vital question as to how far they might be permitted to go in so defending themselves. Christian doctrine certainly narrowed the scope of the permissible, not only in terms of the "other cheek," but also in those of the older Judaic doctrine of misfortune as a trial sent by God's providence to test a man's steadfastness and moral stamina. Certainly prevailing thought was to the effect that it was better to endure than to fight back. A passive and patiently suffering role was enjoined upon the good Christian when faced with the aggressor, and more particularly with an oppressive government. Not only to give Caesar what is Caesar's,—that might be quite all right,—but to give him what he demands without inquiring too closely into his right to demand it, that was seen as the true Christian's proper mode of behavior. It was not only clearly indicated by such sayings as the famous passage in Romans XIII, but also by the actual conduct of countless saints and martyrs.

But there is another strand in the Christian tradition, sug-

[2] Certain broad present-day treatments of this range of issues may be noted here at the outset: Benedetto Croce, *Politics and Morals* (1945); Reinhold Niebuhr, *Christianity and Power Politics* (1940); H. Butterfield, *Christianity and History* (1949); Bertrand de Jouvenel, *Du Pouvoir* (1947); Ludwig Freund, *Politik und Ethik* (1955). Finally, I should like to refer to Gerhard Ritter, *Die Dämonie der Macht* (1947) which is the fifth edition of a work, the several editions of which reflect the distinguished author's evolution in dealing with the problem. It may be doubted however whether his conception of the "demonic" provides any more of a solution than that of the "tragic" in Meinecke's work. See Appendix.

gested in the New Testament and amply developed in some of the Church fathers, notably St. Augustine, which sanctions an aggressive conduct in this world's affairs. This contrasting view appears wherever it becomes a question of the defense of the faith and of the communities which live by the faith. Indeed, by the time St. Augustine faces the problems of a Christian Church, the faith had become fully enthroned as the official religion of the Roman Empire, and as a result its defensive assertiveness had become transformed into a recognition that the Church may ask the secular authorities to draw the sword not only in the defense of the faith, but with the intention of spreading it. This is the heart of the Bishop of Hippo's doctrine of the "just war,"—a war undertaken to create the conditions for converting the heathens, that is to say, for the spreading of the rule of the Holy Empire. Presumably such a war will be conducted with those means which are customary at the particular time and which are at the disposal of the enemy (including atomic bombs).

This contrasting strand of the Christian teachings which preaches just war in the defense and the spread of the faith raises the issue which became later known as that of the "reason of state" in its most acute form. This issue has been customarily treated as peculiarly the problem of Machiavelli and the Machiavellians. But as I shall show, the problem does not even exist for Machiavelli. For only when there is a clash between the commands of an individual ethic of high normativity and the needs and requirements of organizations whose security and survival is at stake can the issue of reason of state become real. For reason of state is nothing but the doctrine that whatever is required to insure the survival of the state must be done by the individuals responsible for it, no matter how repugnant such an act may be to them in their private capacity as decent and moral men. Reason of state is merely a particular form of the general proposition that means must be appropriate to the end, must, in other words, be rational in regard to the end, and that those means are the best which are most rational in the sense of being most likely to succeed. But what is truly rational need not be fully clear, let alone self-evident. In any case, "might makes right."

We find Thucydides struggling with this problem in a characteristic way. In the celebrated discussion between the Athenians and the Melians the Athenians announce the doctrine of this reason of state in no uncertain terms. Might makes right, and "by necessity of their nature, (men) always rule, when they have the power." Justice exists only among equals, and "the powerful exact what they can, while the weak yield what they must." (V, 89.) They had argued the same line in an earlier discussion with the Spartans, though in less striking form. Yet there is a clear indication in Thucydides that he thought this bald doctrine of the Athenians one of the causes of their later difficulties. He then seems to suggest that the treachery which they encountered was the just desert of such cynics. But he does not, of course, by arguing thus, abandon his basic preoccupation with reason of state, as has sometimes been suggested. He merely puts forward the very sensible proposition that a certain amount of pretense, of hypocritical acknowledgment of the values which most members of the community (in this case the Greeks) acknowledge, is part of that "rationality" of means which the doctrine calls for when it enjoins the utmost in exertions on behalf of a given community. Indeed, a moral justification of such hypocrisy may well be argued in some such terms as their value in ensuring survival for a cherished community. But the issue is still relatively easy, when put in terms of patriotism, of the maintenance of an empire, or of a political order which is not itself seen as the essential condition for morality. For an empire is not a moral being in the more elevated sense, which has often, since the ancients, been attributed to the state, and certainly not in the sense in which the Christian Church is. At this point it may be helpful to explore this problem a bit further in relation to the church. For certainly, as an organization, a church faces the problem of survival, of a "reason of church." This "reason of church" was most clearly appreciated by the Jesuits. It is a perplexing issue. To be sure, the issue has not usually been stated in these terms. For those involved in it have well understood the need for camouflage and better still of silence. Pascal's bitter attacks upon the Jesuits, which epitomize objections felt not only by his friends, the Jansenists, but by many other Christians, especially in the Protestant camp, are altogether uncomprehending. For in terms of the individual human being and his salvation, the problem simply does not exist. If it is assumed that organization is not necessary, that we are as well off without a particular organization as with it, naturally anyone in charge of the organization will readily subordinate the requirements of its survival to individual moral considerations. But suppose the organization itself is believed to be essential for the survival of these moral views? Suppose you are convinced that there can be no Christianity without a Christian Church? And suppose further that you believe that the survival of this Church is threatened in the form of rising heretical movements? Then what will be the consequence?

The problems reason of state raises are quite similar. For if the political order is assumed to be an essential condition of a free moral existence, the survival of this order becomes crucial. The old theorists assumed that what was necessary for the security of the state was something not only knowable, but known. To be sure, in their doctrine of the *arcana imperii,* the secrets of empire, of governance or rule, they recognized that this knowledge was difficult to come by and hidden from the common man. In a well-known admonition of James I to his judges, replying to his various critics, he insisted

if there falls out a question of my prerogative or mystery of state, deal not with it, till you consult with the king or his council, or both; for they are transcendent matters . . .
(June 20, 1616, Works (1616) p. 556)

Thus, there were men, kings and their councillors, who did know these secrets, and who therefore could be expected to act rationally, in terms of these secrets. It was a rationality of expedience, of prudence as the older writers called it. If we consult one of the writers of the late sixteenth and early seventeenth century, for example G. Botero, we find that these *arcana* were the sort of thing that the guardians of national security and survival are still stressing and not without justification. At the same time, this *ratio status* covers much that became the content of cameralism: what we nowadays, in their application to public policy, would call the social sciences. In the excitement about these *arcana,* these *rationes status,* there pulses a good deal of the enthusiasm for science which animates so much thought in that period. Of this, more later. At the moment, let us return to the security aspect of the problem, as it presents itself today.

Does this special knowledge, this insight into the "designs of foreigners" (Locke) really solve the problem of determining what is necessary? Admittedly, those carrying on the work of internal and external security know more than others. But how much more? If we consult the records which are available, such as the British Foreign Office documents of the years be-

7

fore the first World War, or the documents which the U.S. State Department has published by way of apology for its conduct of foreign relations between 1933 and 1939, or the numerous records of security investigations in the U.S. and elsewhere, we find again and again the same story: the knowledge of the insiders, of the investigators, administrators and policy makers is woefully inadequate, and certainly did not justify any confidence in their judgment about what constituted the right kind of action, that is to say, the rational road to security and survival.

What is the reason? It is the broad range of contingency in all matters concerning the future course of events, as Aristotle already noted in the *Rhetorics* in defending certain kinds of logical operations in connection with public policy. And it is this contingency which is the basis of the kind of appeal typical of all totalitarian movements which says: "give us the power, and we shall do the rest, don't ask us to explain, we shall take care of you." Free societies are built on the premise that these contingent situations call for broad participation of those affected by them. The usual way of putting it was to pretend that the common man could make just as rational a judgment as the expert. That is to say, the tendency was to exaggerate the rationality of the generality of mankind. But when the contingent nature of political decisions is taken into account, it seems more appropriate to stress the unknown and unknowable elements in the contingent. Such emphasis on the meta-rational environment provides a basis for a "new belief in the common man," for two reasons. One is that where reason's limit is reached, where a plunge into the unknown is necessary, the will of man is engaged, and this not only should be guided, but will be guided by the "higher" rationality of the convictions of the man who acts. The other reason is an expedient one: Since men will usually be more willing to accept the consequences of actions which they themselves helped to decide, the participation of all or most men will provide continuity when the consequences of errors are necessitating change. In short, the fact that much of the environment of man is beyond his rational knowledge places strict limitations upon any reason of state, any *ratio status*. But the issue as such persists. The problem of security and survival calls for some kind of solution. What shall be the guide, the moral law or the requirements of expediency?

We see this problem all around us at the present time, though in a secular form. The key value is freedom. There are those who are convinced that the survival of freedom, of a free community, is vitally threatened by the rise of totalitarianism. First the major threat appeared to be the Hitler dictatorship. In the protracted arguments over what to do the question of war was always involved. Would we Americans be justified, it was asked, in attacking this evil man, this evil organization which threatens our very existence? Or should we even yield to his attacks in order to preserve the peace. The appeasers won, until the attack took the form of physical aggression upon the United States. Whether it was "the wave of the future" or the "managerial revolution" which served as a basis for the pleading,—the underlying notion always was that the United States of America, or Britain, or France was moribund, that in other words the organization was outmoded, was no longer worth defending.

We are in the midst of the argument again at the present time. Quite a few would now argue that it would have been better to resist Hitler at the outset, when he re-armed, when he occupied the Rhineland and so forth, even if they recoil from advocating the desirability of an outright attack, a pre-

9

ventive war. As a result, the United States and her Allies are now pursuing a policy, not of appeasement, but of containment. "Thus far and no farther!" is the battle cry of all those who feel convinced that the survival of the United States of America, and that means her security, as well, is decisively bound up with the survival of freedom and justice. We have therefore arrived at the point which St. Augustine saw, and which the Jesuits faced most clearly, although orthodox teachings throughout the intervening years recognized it, too: the point at which there heaves into view the problem of the clash between moral norms for individual life and those requirements of organization which are occasioned by the weapons an enemy is prepared to employ.

This is the issue which is at the heart of all the bitter arguments over civil liberties. The extreme positions are easily grasped and the land resounds with them. On the one hand there are those who would go to any length to defend the United States against her enemies within and without; on the other hand are those who, regardless of the consequences, would maintain the American belief as embodied in the rights guaranteed by the constitution. The believers in *Fiat justitia, pereat mundus* glare at those who coldly observe that *Inter arma leges silent*. The Republic is being rocked to its very foundations by this controversy. Why? Because the United States, like the churches, is an organization which *rests upon a moral belief*. It is not merely a country that may be right or wrong; its very being is bound up with the maintenance of certain standards. The faith in man which expresses itself in the American bill of rights is one without which the United States of America ceases to be what it has been. It may well go on as a people, and probably would, but its essence would be altered, would be revolutionized.

10

The Communists who maintain this challenge in the modern world are quite frankly believers in a radical rationality of means. Every revolutionary has to be. Karl Marx was quite bland about it. In his opinion, the revolutionary goal of the liberation of the proletariat from its chains was hallowing any means calculated to achieve that end. But for Marx, as for Machiavelli, there was no serious problem involved. Marx, and Lenin following him, was no believer in conventional morality. The individual was for him submerged in the historical process; if he was intelligent, and not too much handicapped by class prejudice, he perceived these historical forces and acted accordingly. That is to say the end did not need to *justify* the means, because the problem of justification only arises when there exists a recognized conception of justice with which the necessary means are in conflict. For Marx, as for Machiavelli, on the other hand, the approach was rigidly instrumentalist and constructivist. This does not mean that Marx or Machiavelli did not cherish an image of man which transcended the given; quite the contrary. Both believed that in the rightly constructed community, human beings will be morally superior. But this is a projection, something to be achieved in the very process which is the primary concern of these thinkers.[3]

When confronted with the real threat of Communist conquest, the bourgeoisie, so-called, has typically reacted by becoming Fascist.[4] Fascism, though varied in its particular ideo-

[3] Cf. James Burnham, *The Machiavellians* (1943) for a present-day view.
[4] The term "bourgeoisie," actually lacks precision, as the phenomena it refers to have undergone historical evolution. It is here meant in the post-Marxist sense of virtually all people who are not classifiable as "proletariat"; to speak of these as a "middle class" is not feasible, since there is no "upper class" above them.

logical content, has invariably taken the position that any means, even the most inhumane forms of violence, calculated to meet and then to destroy the Communist danger, are "justified." Such brutal expressions as Goering's "where one planes, shavings fall" or Gregor Strasser's "yes, legitimate up to the last rung (of the ladder leading to the gallows), but we still shall hang them," are characteristic for this outlook. Similar thought patterns are now common among those who are excited about the Communist danger in the United States. These statements all are basically "reason of state" arguments. The desirability of defending the existing order has come to be taken as self-evident, and hence as a task calling for whatever means are readily at hand. Security and survival are on everyone's lips as the goals in terms of which all political behavior ought to be conducted. The naive surprise with which many editorials nowadays comment upon anyone who questions the total claim made on behalf of security, defense and survival is very revealing.

Is it an accident that the Catholic Church should be so closely associated with these views? Hardly in the light of history. The church has for many centuries known about the problems involved. She has been prepared since the days of St. Augustine to take that horn of the dilemma which says that in fighting the enemy all bars are down, that while at war the laws are silent. The church has been the *Roman* church, and she carries the heritage proudly. It certainly is a position which has "worked" in a worldly way. Perhaps it is all that can be hoped for.

The United States is, however, basically committed to a position different from that of the Catholic Church. It is committed to a faith in the common man, in the capacity of human beings to work together effectively by granting to each member of the Community a substantial amount of freedom, freedom to search out the truth for himself, to argue and to be wrong. The United States is committed, through its constitution, to the proposition that we do not know the truth, except in comparative terms. The final truth is there, but no man or group of men is in possession of it. God is there, but no man or group of men can speak with greater assurance about Him than any other. We know that one proposition may contain more truth than another, but we do not know that this proposition is final, and the presumption is that it is not.

For any community built upon such a faith, the task of survival and of security becomes one of defending *the inner-most self* as well as that of defending *the outer-most boundary,* when confronted with an enemy who manipulates this faith as the Communists do. It is their right, under our assumptions, to claim that their views are more nearly true than ours; but it is not their right to destroy the community which enables them to say so. But how can we stop them from destroying the community? Must we say with Mussolini and Hitler, as well as their latter-day followers, that Communists must be destroyed and that all those who object to their destruction must be destroyed likewise? Must we say that the security and survival of the American community must be achieved, even if it means subverting those very norms and institutions upon which the United States of America rests?

The problem is not peculiar to the United States, though it posits itself here with particular poignancy. The problem has arisen wherever a constitutional order of the libertarian kind has been confronted with the Communist challenge, and with the Fascist response to that challenge. In England and France, in Italy and Germany extended debates have been waged and certain steps have been taken to try to cope with the situation.[5] What we are here concerned with is a body of thought, of searching political thought which bears upon the issue. It is customary to consider the doctrine of the "reason of state" largely in connection with those writers who in the course of the seventeenth, eighteenth and nineteenth centuries have been proponents of power, of autocracy and absolutism, Machiavelli and Bodin, Hobbes, Richelieu, Frederick the Great and Hegel.

But the problem of security and survival faces the constitutional order, faces the government of law, just as much as it does an autocratic government. Hence the deeper thinkers who have developed the political thought of constitutionalism have had to address themselves to this issue. But for them it is a much more perplexing issue. They were caught in the paradox that we have been discussing. Can you justify the violation of the law, when the survival of the legal order is at stake? These thinkers could not proceed on the easy path of arguing from the supreme value of the state, as could be done by Hobbes and others who, following Machiavelli, sanctified order regardless of its justice. The present study is in part the result of a belief in the timeliness of their reflections at the present juncture. His work on Althusius, many years ago, first brought the writer face to face with the issue; it has stayed with him ever since. It is crucial in the Calvinists, in Milton, in Harrington and Locke, in Montesquieu and Kant. The most perplexing "synthesis" finally is achieved by Hegel's dialectic of the constitutional order as the "crowning end" of history. But none of these approaches really provides a solution.

[5] For a few brief remarks, see below, chapter VII. As stated in the preface, it is my hope to return to this subject soon.

Machiavelli

*The State As a Work of Art and
Its Rationality*

IN HIS JUSTLY CELEBRATED STUDY of reason of state, Friedrich Meinecke started with a chapter on Machiavelli. He frankly admitted that Machiavelli had not used the term, but he still felt that Machiavelli was the first who "thought through" the true nature and essence of reason of state. He furthermore felt that this was a historical necessity, because this could only have been done by a "pagan who did not know the terrors of hell, but approached his lifework with the naïveté of classical antiquity." Our view is quite at variance with this position. Meinecke himself points out that classical antiquity never grasped the problem in its true nature, because the ancient Greeks and Romans considered the state the highest value in life, and therefore ethics and political ethics "coincided." While this is only true in general terms, it is correct to say that political practice usually conformed to amoral patterns of expediency. The famous discussion between the Athenians and Melians to which we have already referred brings this out. But it is equally clear,—and Meinecke fails to mention it,—that Thucydides not only realized that the Athenians' bald enunciation of the doctrine that "Might makes right" shocked the

Greek world, but also that this shock hurt the Athenians in later dealings with other Greeks and therefore probably contributed to their defeat.[1] Still and all, the main point is that Machiavelli broadly accepted the view of classical antiquity, namely that the state is the highest value. He was thereby precluded from seeing the issue of the clash between a transcendent morality and the requirements of security and survival of the political order in its more dramatic form. Meinecke himself remarks that Christendom, through the mouth of St. Augustine, passed the final judgment upon the outlook of classical antiquity in stating that *remota justitutia quid sunt regna nisi magna latrocinia,*[2] that is to say that without justice, states (kingdoms) are nothing but great bands of robbers. The Middle Ages lived facing this injunction, and in theory at least, all government was seen as strictly subordinated to law, not only the law of nature, but also customary law on a comprehensive scale. Yet that medieval world had passed from the stage of Italian politics long before Machiavelli came to consider the matter. More especially in the turbulent factionalism of Florence the actions of government were certainly not ruled by any scrupulous regard for law, whether customary or natural. And it is against this background of a cynical condot-

---

[1] Cf. John H. Finley, Jr., *Thucydides* (1942) pp. 103-4 and 208ff., and David Grene, *Man in his Pride* (1950) esp. pp. 56 ff.

[2] It might be mentioned in passing that the phrase *remota justitutia* permits of several interpretations, depending upon whether one takes it to mean if, when *or* since justice is absent; it should also be born in mind that the phrase speaks of *regna* and not of *civitates*. The matter has been in heated dispute between the learned; men like Figgis, McIlwain and the Carlyles having taken markedly divergent views. But whichever way interpreted, there can be no doubt that St. Augustine insisted upon the transcendent morals which his concept of justice implied, oriented as it was toward God and the love which the just man will bear him.

tiere politics that Machiavelli's reflections must, it is generally agreed, be projected. If that is done, it becomes immediately clear that his views are inspired by a deep-felt desire to substitute a higher value for the rampant egoism of the times. Not that Machiavelli was the romantic nationalist, such as Fichte, Hegel and others in the nineteenth century saw fit to describe him. But he was indeed a true Renaissance thinker in that he wished to bring about a rebirth of that spirit of classical antiquity which was manifest in Athenian, Spartan and Roman patriotism. And like other works of the Renaissance, his version was not a mere copy, but was a vitally altered and reformed philosophy of politics: the state is seen as a work of art, rather than as the framework of education for virtue.[3]

This vital alteration and moulding is reflected in his central conception of *virtù*. *Virtù* which is often very misleadingly rendered as "virtue" is in point of fact meant as an antithesis to much that the word virtue implies: its Christian as indeed its Platonic and Judaic connotation.[4] But does this mean that *virtù* is wholly devoid of moral implications? Does it imply a *virtù* from which all notion of virtue is excluded, and stress is laid upon force and force alone? Some have argued that Machiavelli's conception of *virtù* might be summed up in the

[3] This point has been developed by J. H. Whitfield, *Machiavelli* (1947) in a chapter entitled "The Anatomy of Virtue," basing his analysis upon F. Ercole's *La Politica di Machiavelli* (1926), but our own position differs somewhat in seeking positively to identify the grounds of Machiavelli's moral position. Cf. also R. de Mattei, "Fortuna e Virtù del Machiavelli al Lottino" in *Archivio di Storia della Filosofia Italiana*, VII (1938) Fasc. IV.

[4] Among the large number of studies on Machiavelli, one might mention, besides the works noted below, the following: Ettore Janni, *Machiavelli* (1927) (Engl. ed. 1930); H. Butterfield, *The Statecraft of Machiavelli* (1940, 1949); Leonhard von Muzalt, *Machiavelli's Staatsgedanke* (1945); Leonard Olschki, *Machiavelli, the Scientist* (1945); Roberto Ridolfi, *Vita di Niccolò Machiavelli* (1954).

qualities of a successful highway robber or brigand chief.[5]
Actually *virtù* is nowhere definitively defined by Machiavelli. It
is a concept which was quite current in fifteenth century Italy.[6]
It is a complex and somewhat dialectical concept in which
the Christian notions survive through their kinship with Stoic
views which lie embedded in the Roman *virtus*. But Meinecke
is right when he suggests[7] that the concept has a flavor peculiar
to Machiavelli. This probably results from his pre-occupation
with the state as a work of art. *Virtù* thus involves manliness
which means courage and prowess, but also self-discipline and
steadfastness. *Virtù* means a willingness to fight, but also a
willingness to sacrifice oneself for the *patria*. It means a determination to succeed but also a recognition of the civic obligation to serve. In short, *virtù* is, like the Roman *virtus* and the
Greek *areté*,[8] the congeries of qualities required of the citizen
of a constitutional republic such as Athens or Rome in classical antiquity; its nearest modern equivalent is excellence. It
appears from time to time in exceptional degree in an outstanding individual, a hero who possesses the capacity for great
political and military achievements. It is then that a state is
founded or reformed. Thus *virtù* is the kind of excellence
needed in the citizen of a republic and in the ruler and leader
as well. In monarchies it is primarily needed in the ruler. But

[5] Jacques Maritain, *La Fin du Machiavélisme* (1941); G. Toffanin,
Machiavelli e il Tacitismo (1921) and *Il Cinquecento* (1929).
[6] See Ida Wyss, *Virtù und Fortuna bei Boiardo und Ariost* (1931)
and E. E. Cassirer, *Individuum und Kosmos in der Philosophie der
Renaissance* (1927).
[7] Meinecke, op. cit., p. 39 f. Meinecke largely follows the study of
his pupil E. W. Mayer, *Machiavelli's Geschichtsauffassung und sein
Bergriff Virtù* (1912) which Whitfield does not seem to have come across
[8] On the *areté* concept see Werner Jaeger, *Paideia—A Study of
Greek Culture* (1934-44). Jaeger in this renowned study shows the
central position of *areté* in the Greek system of values.

for Machiavelli the focus of interest was that higher *virtù* which characterizes the founder and builder of a state, the man of heroic stature who creates that most extraordinary of all human creations or works of art: a political order. Through such an order the conditions for an ordered and disciplined civic life, a *virtù ordinata,* are created, and thereby both fortune and necessity are mastered.

If the state is thus seen as a work of art, the human beings involved in its creation, as well as other material circumstances and relations are seen in analogy to the clay in the sculptor's hand, to the wood and stone of the architect. They have their material qualities and these qualities are given. Machiavelli sees them as *necessità,* something to be reckoned with and mastered. This notion of a necessity, of laws of nature which must be obeyed by him who would succeed, give the statesman-artist an opportunity for moulding his human material. Machiavelli speaks recurrently of the *necessità ordinata dalle leggi.* Here, too, he is the reviver of classical notions: for the lawgiver in Greek and Roman antiquity, the *nomethetes* of Plato and the *Rector Reipublicae* of Cicero are employing the laws to make men virtuous.[9]

But the world of politics is for Machiavelli not only compounded of *virtù* struggling with *necessità,* of human excellence building a political order in terms of the needs and requirements of such an order and of the obstacles that environment presents, but there must also be recognized the contin-

[9] See *Discorsi,* I, 1 and 6 and II, Introduction as illustrative. Compare in this connection H. Butterfield's *The Statecraft of Machiavelli* (1941) which strikes a sane balance between those who would misinterpret Machiavelli as a perverter of all morals and a glorifier of violence *per se* and those others who would overlook the decisive challenge to all transcendent moral ideals, that is to say transcending the political order, which Machiavelli's views imply.

gent intervention of good or bad luck. *Fortuna,* a Renaissance concept as current as *virtù,* is seen as wholly unpredictable and fortuitous. Machiavelli says that *fortuna* is a woman, and that therefore it is well to be impetuous when dealing with her. "It is necessary, if you wish to master her, to conquer her by force; and it can be seen that she lets herself be overcome by the bold rather than by those who proceed coldly." And in keeping with the views of the time, and presumably his own amatory experiences, he adds: "and therefore, like a woman, she is always a friend to the young, because they are less cautious, fiercer, and master her with greater audacity."[10] About half man's actions are governed by this unpredictable goddess, but the other half man can control, and in Machiavelli's opinion, the less wisdom and valor men possess, the greater is the role of fortune. States will therefore fluctuate less, if a ruler or leader is ready to master fortune. They will continue to fluctuate "until some ruler shall arise who is so great an admirer of antiquity as to be able to govern such states so that Fortune may not have occasion, with every revolution of the sun, to display her influence and power."

It is evident that among these three ideas of *virtù, fortuna* and *necessità* which Machiavelli employs as a central frame of reference for his interpretation of politics, *necessità* is the most novel, though some discussions of *necessità* antedate Machiavelli. But it is this stress upon the harsh realities, the requirements of power and the bitterly felt needs of politics which distinguishes Machiavelli's approach to politics from the preceding medieval and humanist thought. For the stress here, as well as in classical antiquity's philosophers, had been upon what ought to be; in Machiavelli it is upon what is. Many of

[10] See *Prince,* XXV (at end). The role of fortune as discussed in the *Discourses* is well stated in II, 30 (at end) and in III, 9 (at end).

his most shocking remarks, such as the pointed *rebus sic stantibus* doctrine concerning treaties in the eighteenth chapter of *The Prince,* are rooted in this necessity which according to an old adage "knows no law." No law, that is, of a normative kind; political life is ruled by the "laws of necessity."[11] And therefore it behooves the practitioner of the art of politics to study these laws with cold detachment and to act accordingly. The Roman admonition *politica est res dura,*[12] politics is a hard matter, forms the heart of this doctrine.

This doctrine of necessity is the core of Machiavelli's much praised and much abused "scientism." (*Prince* XV.) His works are replete with rigidly factual, existential judgments and of prudential advice based upon them such as "a prince therefore should be slow in undertaking any enterprise upon the representations of exiles, for he will generally gain nothing by it but shame and serious injury." Presumably what holds for a prince, holds for a republic as well. There is no need for dwelling upon this point, often disputed in terms which are derived from present-day aspirations in the social sciences, especially when seen in relation to public policy,[13] for basically Machiavelli's approach to the question is in terms of a naive empiricism which would derive its material from casual observation, unchecked reports and uncritical reading of the writers of

[11] I am reminded here of an incident which is said to have occurred at the commencement of the more radical phase of the English revolution. When some MPs protested at the doors of parliament house against being excluded by Pride's Purge, crying "By what law? By what law?" the sergeant-at-arms replied: "By the law of necessity."

[12] The doctrine is related to the rising emphasis on calculation and accounting in business and statistics, the *Rechenhaftigkeit* which Burckhardt, in *The Culture of the Renaissance* stressed.

[13] See the volume edited by Daniel Lerner and Harold D. Lasswell, *The Policy Sciences* (1952) and the author's review article: "Is Public Policy a Science?" in *Public Policy,* vol. IV (1953).

classical antiquity. (*Disc*. I,6) The results were, as has often been pointed out, most deplorably unscientific: his belief in a citizen army, at a time when there impended a revolution in the military field toward professional armies, his fallacious assessment of the political chances of Cesare Borgia, his recourse to the city state of classical antiquity in a period of rising national territorial states, his notion of the state as a construct, a willful creation rather than the result of forces associated with the growth of national communities and new economic forms, his altogether striking disregard of economic factors,—these are only a few of the numerous illustrations for the highly unscientific nature of his alleged scientism. But the impulse was nonetheless there. Machiavelli wanted to understand the world as it actually is, he was certain that success in politics depends upon such understanding and he tried as best he could to make some progress in that direction.[14]

But the very cast of his thought kept him from "discovering" the problem of the reason of state. Reason of state as a doctrine merely constitutes, as we have said, a particular species of the generic class of behavior or conduct which is rationalized in terms of the means required to achieve a given end. It is incorrect to make an absolute dichotomy, as the school of Max Weber and others tend to do, between this kind of rationality which Weber called *"zweckrational"* and the other

[14] This point has recently been stressed by Leonardo Olschki, *Machiavelli, The Scientist* (1945), but Olschki overestimates both the novelty and the success of Machiavelli. He overlooks the extent to which the type of question which he claims to be wholly novel had been dealt with by Aristotle and Polybius, *inter alias*. Nor is it clear why he should on the one hand say that Machiavelli is not an empiricist, yet on the other stress that he was essentially basing his conclusion on practical observation, rather than classical and humanist learning. It would seem that Felix Gilbert's approach,—which Olschki rejects,—is sounder, as put forward in "The Humanist Concept of the Prince" in *The Journal of Modern History*, XI, (1939). See also A. H. Gilbert, *Machiavelli's Prince and its Forerunners* (1938).

kind which reasons about values or ends which Weber called *"wertrational."* The reason is that means and ends cannot be thus kept in two wholly separate, and mutually exclusive boxes. Not only can means become ends, and ends means, as Weber recognized, but in many cases the one is so definitely implied in the other that they cannot be thought about as apart from each other. Machiavelli's approach offers a good illustration for this aspect of the matter, in that his view of the state (when he means the government or the political order by it) invests the state with such paramount value that it becomes the source of all other values. The state is for Machiavelli the supreme and all-inclusive good and therefore no genuine good can be found outside the state. As a result, Machiavelli sees no need for "justifying" the means which are required for building and maintaining a state. The state's security and survival are *"hors de discussion."* Consequently, we might say that it is self-justifying as any absolute value is (for that is presumably what absolute means). It is, in this connection, interesting to note that some of the passages in which Machiavelli is said to have expounded the infamous doctrine that the end justifies the means,—an interpretation which is so general that it has led translators to impute it to Machiavelli when the plain purport of the words is quite different,—actually merely state that men tend to behave in such a way as to achieve their ends. Thus the passage at the end of chapter eighteen of *The Prince* which is customarily translated as "the end justifies the means," says in the original that *attioni degli uomini . . . si guarda al fine,* an entirely reasonable proposition. For Machiavelli, in short, the problem of reason of state does not exist in its more pointed and typical form, because the necessity of acting in accordance with the state's requirements needs no justification.[15]

[15] In his learned commentary on Machiavelli's *Discourses,* Leslie J. Walker discusses the matter in a contrary sense, although he agrees

For those who later in the century came to expound the doctrine of the reason of state, more especially Giovanni Botero, who is credited with inventing the term,[16] the problem presented itself how such conduct as would rationally be required for the survival and security of the state might be "justified" within the context of Christian morality. For only those who had abandoned once again the idea that the political order is the source of all true value, and had through reformation or counterreformation been re-confirmed in their belief in a transcendental source of moral judgments, were confronted with the problem of "justification." Reason of state in this perspective is the doctrine by which organizational requirements are fitted into the value system of Christian morals. But it is defined by Botero as the knowledge of the means which are suited to found a state, to maintain it and to enlarge it.[17]

When seen in this perspective, the position of Machiavelli can be further illuminated by considering finally the question of the role of religion, as seen by Machiavelli. Many have either

---

that the doctrine that the end justifies the means has no place in *The Prince*. He cites, however, *Discourses* I,9,3 in support of the contention that Machiavelli espouses the doctrine here. But what does Machiavelli say? "Conviene bene, che, accusandolo il fatto, lo effetto lo scusi; e quando sia buono . . . sempre lo scuserà." But excusing is not justifying, but almost the opposite. See *The Discourses of Niccolò Machiavelli* (1950) pp. 118 ff. Machiavelli is here talking of "racconciare" or mending, of reforming a system. Significantly, and in keeping with his general outlook, he goes on to comment on the danger, in a monarchy, of a successor using the power he has inherited *ambiziosamente* rather than *virtuosamente*.

[16] See *Della Ragion di Stato* (1589) and in Latin *De Ratione Status* (1666) passim. Meinecke says nicely concerning Botero that his doctrine "represents a richly ornamented Jesuit church, developed out of the Renaissance style" which satisfied the friends of Spain and the Holy See as well as the admirers of the republic of Venice.

[17] Cf. our definition above ch. I, p. 4, for contrast.

assumed or argued from certain well-known passages that Machiavelli is a "pagan" in the sense that religion has purely heuristic value for him. Machiavelli might, from this view-point, have agreed with Marx that religion is the opium of the people. In point of fact, Machiavelli displays a very marked interest in religion. He notes at the outset in the *Discourses* that the greatness of Rome was due to her religious tradition, and he puts the founders of a religion at the very top of human beings. Indeed, he phrases the latter thought in such a way that one can become doubtful about the position of Machiavelli re-garding the supreme value of the State. At the beginning of chapter X he writes:

Of all men who have been eulogized, those deserve it most who have been the authors and founders of religions; next come such as have established republics and kingdoms . . . On the contrary, those are doomed to infamy and universal execration who have destroyed religions, who have overturned republics and king-doms, . . .

Not only is it difficult to believe that the man who wrote these passages desired for himself the title of a destroyer of the Christian religion, but one is obliged to wonder whether re-ligion is not, after all, assigned a superior rank in the scale of values and whether transcendental morals is not thereby re-enthroned. But this passage speaks actually of public opinion, not of Machiavelli's. And Machiavelli thereafter does not con-cern himself further with the problems of religion which he would have done, if religion embodied what to him was the primary value. Quite on the contrary, he discusses both the religion of the Romans and contemporary events in such terms as to suggest that the value of religion itself is due to its vital importance for a well-ordered state. Machiavelli might well have written the royalist slogan "no bishop, no king," but he would still have thought that it was the maintenance of the kingdom that was the primary consideration. Religion is an instrument, albeit a very important one:

Princes and republics who wish to maintain themselves free from corruption must above all things preserve the purity of all religious observances, and treat them with proper reverence; for there is no greater indication of the ruin of a country than to see religion contemned. (*Discourses* 1,12)

The Protestant perspective on reason of state (to be discussed in the next chapter) may serve to open up a dimension of Machiavelli's thought which links him to the constitutional theorists with whose thought on survival and security we are primarily concerned. But more important unquestionably is the Roman Republican tradition. For to the extent that Machiavelli is inclined to look upon the Roman Republic as the ideal state which a hero embodying *virtù* might expect to realize, he is bound to find himself, as he recurrently does, confronted with a conflict between the type of virtue which the Romans, and more especially the Stoics were stressing and the requirements which the state's security and survival posit. In a very interesting passage in the *Discourses* (I, 10) Machiavelli indicates this problem in commenting upon Caesar:

Nor let anyone be deceived by the glory of that Caesar who has been so much celebrated by writers; for those who praised him were corrupted by his fortune, and frightened by the long duration of the empire that was maintained under his name, *and which did not permit writers to speak of him with freedom*. . . . Caesar is as much more to be condemned, as he who commits an evil deed is more guilty than he who merely has the evil intention . . . Let him also note how much more praise those emperors merited who . . . conformed to the laws like good princes, than those who took the opposite course . . . (Italics mine.)

In elaborating upon this theme, Machiavelli shows clearly that he not only recognized a moral element in the qualities of excellence to be demanded of a prince, but that he attributed survival value to it; for these emperors, he says, did not need legions to defend them, "because they were protected by their own good conduct, the good will of the people and the love of the senate." The Neros, on the other hand, being criminals, were not even protected by all the armies in the world. It seems highly significant that Machiavelli speaks here of criminals, *scellerati,* and that he elaborates on this theme in terms specifically of *sicurtà,* security. He relates this contrast to the statistics about assassination and notes that wicked princes more frequently die by violence. It is clear from such passages as these that virtue in the higher moral sense is recognized by Machiavelli as a genuine achievement, and of real value. Yet such virtue must not be allowed to interfere with the work of the architect who builds or maintains or rebuilds a state. The normativity of the moral norms finds its boundary in the requirements of what the artist builder needs for his work. Here it would seem that nothing is wrong, except what is inexpedient, what will not work. Just as the builder will fashion his materials to suit his purpose, so the statesman, the founder, lawgiver and builder of a state will handle his human material on strictly operational grounds, that is to say, with strict regard to success. Since the state is man's greatest, noblest, most magnificent work, since the state requires man's most creative art, the artist engaged in this enterprise will act with strict regard to the end: *attioni degli uomini si guarda al fine.*

But Machiavelli does not stop at this general point, but recognizes the problems of security and survival of the constitutional order. He grasps the dangers to such an order itself which result from this problem. And how could it have been otherwise, considering his experiences in Florence and his close study of the Roman constitution?[18] But in spite of his

---

[18] On Machiavelli's environment, the most interesting recent study, and a remarkable one, indeed, is Rudolf von Albertini, *Das Florentin-*

sharp criticism of the abuse of the institution of the dictatorship by Marius, Sylla and more especially Caesar, Machiavelli
has nothing better to suggest than such a constitutional dictatorship. In two chapters of the *Discourses,* he addresses himself to the proposition that "the authority of the dictatorship
has always proved beneficial to Rome, and never injurious."[19]
He specifically rejects those writers who "have blamed the
Romans who first introduced the practice of creating dictators
as being calculated in time to lead to despotism in Rome."
Such a view is in his opinion the result of superficial study;
"neither the name nor the rank of the dictator subjected Rome
to servitude, but the authority which citizens usurped to per-
petuate themselves in the government." If this title had not
been available, then another one would have served; for
"power can easily take a name, but a name cannot give
power" (*perchè e'sono le forze che facilmente s'acquistano i
nomi, non i nomi le forza).* What really caused the trouble was
the usurpation and the fact that the attachment to the constitutional order had become so weak as to make such an usurpation possible; for whenever the dictator was appointed "according to public law" he benefited the republic. He gives
several reasons for this. First, the constitutional dictator was
appointed for a limited term only. Secondly, the power of a
dictator was restricted to removing a particular emergency.
Thirdly, the dictator could not alter the constitutional order
itself, abolish existing institutions (*ordini*) or create new ones.

---

ische Staatsbewusstsein im Übergang von der Republik zum Prinzipat
(1955), especially pp. 15-90. See also the newest detailed biography
of Machiavelli by Roberto Ridolfi, *Vita di Niccolò Machiavelli* (1954),
passim. Felix Gilbert's "Bernardo Rucellai and the Orti Oricellari" in
Journal of the Warburg and Courtauld Institute, X (1949), is very
valuable on Machiavelli's relations to the "Republicans."

[19] *Discourses,* I, 34 and 35.

Fourthly, the appointment of the dictator was precisely circumscribed by the constitution itself (and besides the Roman method was a very wise one, he thought). When these conditions were fulfilled, and as long as "the Roman people were not yet corrupted"—a vital condition, indeed!—the institution of the dictatorship was beneficial. Machiavelli goes so far as to claim that this institution was among those essential to Rome's greatness. Without it, Rome would with difficulty have escaped extraordinary emergencies; he mentions the slowness with which regular constitutional arrangements work, because of the division of power among several bodies. As a parallel, Machiavelli suggests the emergency powers of the Venetian Council of Ten. If a republic lacks some such system, it will either have to disregard the constitutional order or perish. And it is essential that in a well-ordered system there be no need for recourse to extraordinary (that is to say extra-constitutional) measures: for such measures are apt to create a pernicious precedent. Further to buttress his argument, he contrasts the *dictator's* office with that of the *Decemvirs,* and he shows how the latter, appointed for longer periods and with undefined powers, were able to convert a conferred authority into an usurped one which make them "tyrants." The dictators, clearly confined to dealing with a particular situation in a limited period and under the supervision of the established constitutional authorities could not do that.[20]

All in all, we find Machiavelli clearly aware of the problem, in its more general connotation, and content to advocate the Roman solution for it, namely a constitutional dictatorship.

[20] For the application of these reflections to contemporary constitutional systems, see C. J. Friedrich, *Constitutional Government and Democracy* (1941 and 1950) last chapter, and the literature cited there. See also below chapter VII.

This sort of approach does not, of course, help with the creeping paralysis of what Machiavelli considered simply "corruption." This to him was a "natural" process, beyond the power of man to cope with.

If it were our purpose to explore the general development of the idea of reason of state, one would now want to turn to Giovanni Botero who perhaps invented and certainly popularized the term, and who as we said above, sought to "justify" such reason of state within the context of Christian morals. But since we are here principally concerned with those writers who were "constitutionalists" and as such believed in a government of laws and not of men, we must leave these predominantly absolutist trends aside. We may, however, be justified in adding a few comments on the large number of Italian writers who, following Botero, developed the doctrine of reason of state in its various dimensions.[21]

In the course of their protracted discussions, reason of state gradually came to be identified with politics, because all the problems of politics have a bearing upon reason of state. Reason of state comprises all that is worth knowing about the state, that is to say, politics.[22] At the same time, the concept lost all its peculiar poignancy in such propositions as that it

[21] Extracts from some of these writers were offered by B. Croce and S. Caramella, *Politici et Moralisti del Seicento—Strada—Zuccolo—Settala—Accetto—Brignole Sale—Malvezzi* (1930); these and others have been the subject of numerous papers (see note 26 at end) by Rudolfo de Mattei, by far the most learned student of this literature in Italian. I owe to Professor Mattei's remarkable private collection the opportunity of consulting quite a few of these works.

[22] Mattei cites Cardinal de Luca as follows: "Questa parola *Politica* è sinonima, e dinota l'istesso che *la Ragione di Stato*, posciaché la parola 'ragione' abbraccia tutto quello che di giusto e di ragionevole dalle leggi Divina, naturale, delle genti, positiva e di convenienza si dispone ovvero si richiede anche tra privati . . ." Giovanni Battista de Luca, *Il Principe Cristiano Pratico* (1680) pp. 66/7 as cited in R. de

is not to be distinguished from civil prudence. "True reason
of state is not different from civil prudence . . . it is not uncon-
nected with moral virtue, nor with religion . . . it is the true
rule of government . . ." Indeed man is born to it[23]

In some of these writers, the idea that every form of government has its proper "reason of state" comes to the fore which
later plays a role in the work of Harrington and more particularly Montesquieu. "To act in accordance with reason of state
does not mean anything else but acting in conformity with the
essence and form of that state which man has decided either
to preserve or to establish . . . all reason of state revolves
around the knowledge of the means . . . which are opportune
for ordering or preserving a particular kind of constitution
of the republic whatever it may be."[24] In him as well as other

---

Mattei, "La Posizione Dottrinale del Botero e le Recenti Interpretazioni
Critiche" in *Bollettino della Società per gli Studi Storici, Archeologici
ed Artistici nella Provincia di Cuneo* (1954) pp. 29 ff. and 49.

[23] Federigo Bonaventura (1555-1602), *Della Ragion di Stato e della
Prudenza Politica* (1601; 1623) Preface. He, as well as Ludovico Settala
(1555-1633) and many others follow Botero in trying to distinguish
between a "good" and a "bad" reason of state, depending on whether
the prince is good or a tyrant. This leads to the paradoxical position
that a good man may more justifiably do bad things than a bad one.
[24] Ludovico Zuccolo (1568?-1630?), *Considerazioni Politiche e Morali
sopra Cento Oracoli d'Illustria Personaggi Antichi* (1623), esp. Oracolo
XI, pp. 54-73. The passage is found in Croce's reprint, pp. 27/8.
A similar distinction was developed by Scipione Chiaramonte (da
Ossena) who in his treatise on reason of state (printed 1635) elaborates
the differentiations, distinguishing 10 meanings of *ragione* and two of
stato (the land and people or the rulers and form of government). He
obviously is making a sort of digest of earlier views, pointing out the
contradictions in speaking of reason of state as good or bad, conclud-
ing that it is both good and bad, true and apparent. He finally differ-
entiates six kinds of *ragion di stato*. Chiaramonte also clearly sets down
the fact that one cannot contrast law and reason of state by assigning
to the former the determinate rules. "Io nego non aver la ragion di

writers of this school, a strongly utilitarian aspect of reason of state arguments is noticeable, foreshadowing Hobbes, Hume and Bentham. This utilitarianism has, of course, Stoic and medieval roots. In any case, once reason of state is recognized as the rational means for maintaining a constitutional order, the road is opened toward a specific republican constitutional reason of state. It would be too much to expect such a development in these sixteenth and seventeenth century Italians. Suffice it to note that they were much concerned to show that a constitutional democracy such as Athens had its brutal side. Time and again it is pointed out that ostracism in such a state might be a rational means for preserving the political order. Nor is this their preoccupation to be wondered at when one remembers that after all Machiavelli's deeper attachment was to such a constitutional order, and hence his effort to discover rules of rational conduct were more particularly focused on such a state's survival. But as we have seen Machiavelli did not elaborate an institutional or behavioral model as a solution to this problem.[25]

In conclusion, it is fair to say that Machiavelli and the Machiavellians and Anti-machiavellians had, in laying bare the hard core of how to conduct governmental affairs rationally and in accordance with scientific knowledge and under-

---

stato materia determinata et regola determinata." When things change, other rules apply, but ragion di stato consists of very definite rules. At times, these may even take the form of law, "ma non sempre è legge: perchè ella è anco fallenza di legge, oltre che non ogni regola di ragion di stato sarà espressamente commandata dalla legge." Here the thought of Chiaramonte comes close to that of English writers on the prerogative. See pp. 82 f. below.

[25] Very interesting specific suggestions can be gleaned from Rudolf von Albertini's *Das Florentinische Staatsbewusstsein im Übergang von der Republik zum Prinzipat* (1955) where the institutional setting of Machiavelli's thought is presented.

standing, touched upon the problem of an immanent conflict, an antinomy involved in the security and survival requirements of a republican (that is to say, a constitutional) government. But the introduction of the problem of a conflict between it and the transcendental norms of an ethic derived from a revealed religion had soon obscured the true nature of this issue, even though Machiavelli himself had vaguely seen and dimly perceived it.[26]

It required a more favorable institutional setting, and an extended process of constitutional development for these issues to crystallize into at least partial answers.

[26] The most penetrating guide to all this mass of literature is contained in a series of articles, published by Rudolfo de Mattei, under the general title of "Il Problema della 'Ragion di Stato' nel Seicento" in *Rivista Internazionale di Filosofia del Diritto.* 1949, 187-210; 1950, 25-38; 1951, 333-356, and 705-723; 1952, 1-19; 1953, 445-461; 1954, 370-384, and 369-383, dealing successively with (1) general problems, (2) origins, (3) Botero, (4) Objections and corrections, (5) Zuccolo, (6) Ammirato, (7) prudence, (8) complete denials, and (9) Jus publicum. It is to be hoped that Professor de Mattei will be able to pull these fine studies together into a book on the problem of reason of state in sixteenth century Italy. I should like to add the following studies by Mattei: L'idea Democratica e Contrattualista negli Scrittori Politici Italiani del Seicento" in *Rivista Storica Italiana,* LX (1948) pp. 1-51; "La Teoria dello 'Stato Misto' nel Dottrinarismo del Seicento" in *Rivista di Studi Politici Internazionali* (1948) pp. 406-436, and "Politica e Morale prima di Machiavelli" in *Giornale Critico della Filosofia Italiana* (1950) pp. 56-67.

III   Survivalists

*The Secular: Harrington, Spinoza,
Montesquieu*

THE DOMINANT MACHIAVELLIAN TRADITION, treated so admirably by Meinecke, became absolutist and monarchial. The problem of these writers was that of fitting the rationale of power of the national, bureaucratic state into a transcendent Christian ethic, whether Catholic or Protestant. As we have seen, Giovanni Botero opened the procession and gave currency to the term. A vast school of Italian writers thereafter explored the issue in all its ramifications. Some saw that the problems of security and survival are not limited to the monarchical and absolute state, that they confront the constitutional government of laws, too. Here security and survival give rise to problems of a much more perplexing sort, as we sketched them in our introductory chapter. Machiavelli skipped over these problems lightly, because in spite of his enthusiasm for the Roman republic, he did not have a secure grasp of the principles of constitutionalism and more especially of its legal foundations. The great writers of the constitutional tradition, and more particularly those who grasped the implications of Machiavelli's skeptical challenge, try, however, to come to grips with these issues in a variety of ways. It is these thinkers with whom I propose to deal in the following chapters, Harrington, Spinoza and Montesquieu, Rousseau, Althusius, Locke and Kant.

They fall into two groups, the "pagans" and the "Christians," for whom the problem posits itself in rather divergent terms. I am using the term "pagan" in that rather limited sense, in which it denotes a writer who acknowledges the Christian religion as a source of virtue, yet makes the political requirements of the state primary and predominant. In such thinkers, secular reasoning and understanding has taken the place of revelation. Any transcendent source of virtue, and more especially of civic virtue, has become attenuated or has disappeared. Harrington, Spinoza, Montesquieu and Hegel are striking representatives of this outlook.

James Harrington (1611-1677)[1] at the very end of his *System of Politics,* which is the last of his works (and incomplete), remarks that "neither Hippocrates nor Machiavelli introduced diseases into man's body nor corruption into government, which were before their times; and seeing they do but discover them, it must be confessed that so much as they have done tends not to the increase but the cure of them, which is the truth of these two authors."[2] What Machiavelli was writing about in *The Prince* was, according to Harrington, the reason of state of a tyranny. Every form of state, including a constitutional democracy, has its own "reason," and such rea-

---

[1] For Harrington, see H. F. Russell Smith, *Harrington and His Oceana* . . . (1914), the standard biography, and Charles Blitzer's *The Political Thought of James Harrington,* a Harvard dissertation (1952), soon to be published by the Yale University Press, gives an extended bibliography.

[2] In John Toland's edition of *The Works of James Harrington* (1700) p. 514. Page references will be to this edition, but the *System* is also reprinted in Charles Blitzer's *The Political Writings of James Harrington* (1955).

son has an external and internal aspect. Externally, it is concerned with maintaining a balance so that it may expand, or at least not be "gained upon." Internally it consists of maintaining its "form," that is to say, its basic institutions intact, provided the internal structure is sound; if it should be unsound, then reason of state would be directed toward their "being mended."

Harrington is very optimistic about reason of state in a democracy. Democracy has an easy time in its foreign relations, because it is so strong, "a good democracy weighing two or three of the greatest princes." Internally, all it needs to do is to prevent the concentration (accumulation) of power. This, however, is only true in a well-structured democracy, whereas if the rich and the poor, the nobility and the populace are in rivalry, "it comes to utter ruin." The reference is, of course, to Rome.

In his major work, *Oceana,* Harrington was somewhat less confident. In fact, he made very special provision for the exercise of emergency powers. Here he develops the idea of constitutional dictatorship. Following the Roman precedent, he provides a specific institutional safeguard. Under the 19th Order (these "orders" in *Oceana* are actually embodying the constitution of the state of Oceana) Harrington empowers the regular legislative bodies to set up a council to deal with threats to security and survival which he calls the Dictatorian (sic!) power. It is composed of the council of war and nine more knights, is strictly limited as to time and persons for which it is competent, and remains subject to control by revocation. It can take all necessary measures including levies; it can make laws, but only for a year, and these must be revoked, when the regular legislature demands it. This council can do all that is necessary in order to defend the established order; it must not subvert it in any way. Harrington explains that he decided upon a council or committee for the exercise of these vast powers, because of the abuse made of individual dictatorship in the closing years of the Roman republic.[3] It is clear that he saw the problem of internal as well as external security and tried to cope with it in a way that would not corrupt the order itself.

In this connection, it is equally clear that Harrington was prepared to allow considerable latitude, as far as any moral restraints are concerned. In defending Machiavelli against the charge of having allowed immoral actions, when the security and survival of the state are at issue, he admits that perhaps Machiavelli went a bit far in the way he put it. "As to the manner of expression it is crudely spoken. But to imagine that a nation will devote itself to death or destruction any more upon faith given or an engagement thereto tending, than if there had been no such engagement made or faith given, were no piety but folly."[4] In short, as even Thomas Aquinas was prepared to allow, "necessity is not subject to law."[5]

But the problem of "reason of state" here involved is still further elaborated by Harrington. Aside from embodying the task of maintaining the system of government intact, reason of state is broadly defined by Harrington as the "administration of the government" or what in a family is called "the main chance." It is concerned, in other words, with growth and perfection. In this connection, Harrington tries to differentiate between good and bad reason of state, depending upon the

[3] Op. cit., pp. 128-30. (On pp. 130 and 319 he adduces the Council of Ten of Venice as precedent. For the Council of Ten, which was a "security council" indeed, see Horatio Brown, *Studies in Venetian History*, I, 76/7.)
[4] Op. cit., p. 509.
[5] *Summa Theologica*, II, I, 96, 6 (end of *respondeo*).

nature of the state which it serves. In order fully to appreciate his viewpoint, one must take into account his marked preference for the political outlook of the ancients which he embodied into his doctrine of the "ancient prudence" as contrasted with "modern prudence." Ancient prudence is "the policy of a commonwealth" while modern prudence is "the policy of King, Lords and Commons." The former was expounded by the ancients and more especially Aristotle, while modern prudence was derived from the Goths and Vandals, and has come to dominate the West, but has deteriorated into pure lordly rule. To put this line of analysis into the terms of our own discussion, we could say that ancient prudence involves constitutional reason of state, while modern prudence embodies absolutist reason of state. Among modern writers, Machiavelli would then be expounding ancient prudence, while Hobbes advocates modern prudence.[6] Both face the problem of political rationality in tough-minded terms of the security and survival of the political order. Both see it as a scientific problem of fashioning the tools, the effective means for the maintenance of order and government, but Machiavelli more especially appreciates the problem as that of constitutional systems.[7] Harrington, in elaborating the constitution of a balanced commonwealth, made a valiant effort to apply what he conceived to be Machiavelli's realistic principles[8] to the

[6] It is noteworthy to what an extent Harrington is concerned with combatting Hobbes and his geometrical method (though he highly esteemed him); cf. Blitzer, loc. cit., p. XXVII/XXVIII. In this connection, compare Hume's judgment that Harrington's was "the only valuable model of a commonwealth that has yet been offered to the public." Cf. "Idea of a Perfect Commonwealth" in *Political Essays*.

[7] All of Harrington's interesting application of this notion which leads him to the discovery of the "balance" of classes and of the power that is derived from property, and more especially landed property, must here remain undiscussed. Cf. Blitzer, op. cit., passim.

[8] No writer is more constantly referred to than Machiavelli by the

building of a constitutional order. Like Machiavelli, he considered the building of a commonwealth the highest achievement of man: "in the Art of Man (being the imitation of nature, which is the Art of God) there is nothing so like the first call of beautiful order out of chaos and confusion as the architecture of a well-ordered commonwealth." And among the essentials of such a structure, he considered a special organ to handle internal and external security with secrecy and dispatch to be of decisive importance. Whether he fully appreciated the dangers, his enthusiasm for the Council of Ten of Venice, that infamous model of all secret police set-ups, makes one more than doubtful. But he certainly stressed the importance of two crucial points: (1) that such an organ must not be permanent,[9] and (2) that it ought to be separate from the regular magistrates,—both principles which tend to be overlooked not only in the handling of the emergency power in constitutional systems, but more particularly in the administration of security programs today.

If Machiavelli and Harrington were concerned with political liberty, trying to find an effective institutional substructure, so was Baruch Spinoza (1632-1677). But like the great philosopher that he was he saw the central problem as that of placing the organization of power within the broader context of nature. He took the bold line of proclaiming the complete identity of power or might with law and right. That "the big

---

author of *Oceana,* and usually in the sense of empirical realism; he is a number of times put alongside Dr. Harvey, as in the citation adduced below.

[9] Harrington (p. 319) quotes Livius: "maxima libertatis custodia est, ut magna imperia diuturna non sint, et temporis modus imponatur, quibus juris imponi non potest," and observes that this principle applies especially to a dictator; again he adds that this is also the view of Machiavelli who in his Discourses, Book III, ch. 24, analyses the collapse of the Roman republic in some such terms, more especially referring to Marius, Sylla and Caesar. Cf. also p. 443.

fish devour the little fish by natural law and right" is the cruel doctrine resulting from this premise. If that were all, we could leave Spinoza aside, as we do Hobbes and other absolutists. But Spinoza, even though he knows of no separation or balance of powers, "limits" the power of government by the residual power of the subjects who retain a will to be free. And this determination to be free possesses an indelible, hard core: the freedom to think and to believe. It is the recognition of this basic freedom of one's convictions which places Spinoza among the constitutionalists. At the same time, his rigorous insistence upon the role of power makes the problem of the security and survival of the political order unavoidable. Hence within the general context of Spinoza's philosophy, the problem of democratic freedom, as contrasted with the requirements of reason of state, has particular poignancy.

Spinoza's radically naturalistic doctrine of power thus made him espouse a constitutional system, a government of laws of an aristocratic kind because of his realistic appraisal of men's will to be free.[10] In this his concern with liberty, he, too, acknowledges his deep indebtedness to Machiavelli. In his *Political Treatise* (E I, 315) he calls him that "most ingenious man" and that "most far-seeing man." He fully recognizes that "he was favorable to liberty for the maintenance of which he has besides given the most wholesome advice."[11] But since

[10] Spinoza's works are most readily accessible in English in R. H. M. Elwes' edition *The Chief Works of Benedict de Spinoza* (rev. ed. 1900); For the Latin originals I used Vloten's and Land's *Benedicti de Spinoza's Opera* (1913). Page references in the following notes are to these editions, prefixed by either E or L. I have, however, at times altered the translation, where clarity seemed to require it. Among commentaries most important for our purpose are Jakob Freudenthal, *Spinoza, Leben und Lehre* (1927), H. A. Wolfson, *The Philosophy of Spinoza* (1934) and Leo Strauss, *Die Religionskritik Spinozas* (1930).

[11] See also Leo Strauss, op. cit., p. 218. Cf. on liberty, especially Ch. XX of the *Theologico-Political Treatise*.

Spinoza, like Machiavelli, submerges the problem of right in that of power, can there be any problem of "reason of state"? The question touches the foundation of Spinoza's ethics.

This is not the place to develop Spinoza's complex system in which scientific rationalism is "boldly combined" with pantheistic deification of nature. Disciplined ethical behavior is the "natural" consequence of man's reason with which he reaches out for that perfect rational existence which is God's. This development of man's power does not constitute self-denial at all. Not asceticism, but the higher self-fulfillment of freedom is the end of human existence. To say it in Spinoza's own words:

Every man exists by the highest law and right of nature, and consequently by this same right he does what follows from the necessity of his own nature; thus by the highest right and law of nature every man judges what is good and what is bad, and consults his own advantage as he thinks best, revenges himself, and tries to preserve what he loves and to destroy what he hates. Now if men lived according to the guidance of reason, every man would enjoy his right without injury to another.[12]

This being so, man needs the coercive frame of a political order, a *civitas* or state which is the rational order through which man's passions are effectively controlled by laws and penalties. Only within such a state do the violations of the commands of reason which passions induce man to commit become crimes (*peccatum*); good and bad are defined only within the *civitas* by "common consent." In all of this is involved Spinoza's firm conviction that "man is then the most independent, when he is most led by reason."[13]

[12] E. II, p. 213/4—*Ethics* IV, Prop. XXXVII, Schol. II. The above translation is much revised.

[13] E. I, pp. 294 and 313. Spinoza's conviction rests upon his notion that "God who exists in absolute liberty, also understands and operates of necessity, that is, exists, understands, and operates according to the necessity of his own nature." *Ibid.*

What, then, is the best commonwealth like? The fact that Spinoza left the *Political Treatise* unfinished prevents a firm answer. There are, however, fairly clear indications that he favored a constitutional republic, that is to say a government of laws and not of men. One thing is certain, namely, that that commonwealth is most powerful and independent which is founded and guided by reason. What this means, concretely, is that "that rule (*imperium*) is the best where men live their lives in concord, and where rights (*jura*) are kept inviolate."[14] This can actually be the case only in a commonwealth which the multitude has freely instituted. Spinoza insists on this even though he frankly insists likewise that "as the wise man has a complete right to do all that reason dictates . . . so also the foolish and ignorant man has a complete right to do all that desire dictates . . ." "all men are born ignorant . . . nevertheless . . . they are no more bound to live by the dictates of an enlightened mind, than a cat is bound to live by the laws of the nature of a lion." That is to say, nature does not forbid people to live according to their desires and passions. Quite the opposite. It forbids neither strife nor hatred, nor anger, nor deceit. For nature is much wider than human reason; yet no one can deny that "it is much better for us to live according to the laws and assured dictates of reason." Hence man's readiness to enter into society. But this entrance into society which can be described in terms of the model of a contract[15] does not imply the surrender of all his natural rights; for any compact

---

[14] L. II, p. 23 (*Tract, Pol.* V, 2); cf. also E. I, p. 303.

[15] Spinoza, unlike Hobbes and many others, treats the contract as a pure construction to make explicit what is implicit in the slow evolution of mankind, as is shown by his discussion both in the *Political Treatise* and in the *Theologico-Political Treatise*. The decisive discussion in the latter occurs in chapter XVI, upon which the above is largely based. See E. I, pp. 200 ff.

is valid only within the limits of its utility to him who makes it. Spinoza is relentless in this respect: Everyone has by nature a right to act deceitfully (*dolo*) nor is he bound to observe a contract, except by the hope of a greater good or the fear of a greater evil than would result from the breaking of the contract! This follows inexorably from the premise that everyone's right extends as far as his power. For this very reason, democracy is best; it may be defined as a society "which wields all its power as a whole." In it, the citizens have gone farthest in surrendering all their power, and hence "they are obliged to fulfill the commands of the highest power, however absurd they may be, else they will be public enemies, and will act against reason which urges the preservation of the *civitas*, of the state, as a primary duty." There is slight danger, Spinoza thinks, that thoroughly absurd commands will be given in a democracy: it is "almost impossible that the majority of a people, especially if it be a large one, decide upon an absurd command."[16] In any case, that state is the most free whose laws are founded on sound reason, and where all share in the making of the laws; considering that they all seek self-preservation and peace, this goal will most likely be realized in such a state. And Spinoza concludes:

I think I have now shown sufficiently clearly the basis of a democracy: I have especially desired to do so, for I believe it of all forms of government the most natural, and the most consonant with individual liberty.[17]

Here everyone hands over his natural rights only to the majority of which he is a member. "Thus all remain, as they were in the state of nature, equals."

[16] E. I, p. 206.
[17] E. I, p. 207. *Theol.-Pol. Tr.* Ch. XVI.

Within this broad context, Spinoza vindicates a fairly radical reason of state. If placed within the framework of our present problems, it is pretty clear that Spinoza would be prepared to accept whatever the community decided to do about its own security and survival. "No one in possession of power ought to abide by his promises to the injury of his dominion." But I believe he would also argue that there was not any too great danger that a free people would permanently deprive itself of the kinds of benefits which a bill of rights was intended to bestow upon them. In the final analysis, though, it would be the majority, preferably a constitutional majority, which would have the "last word." For Spinoza, the requirements of the commonwealth are over-riding. There cannot be any doubt about the proposition that "reason altogether teaches to seek peace, and peace cannot be maintained, unless the commonwealths' general laws be kept unbroken." (III, 6) And further, "wherefore, if a man who is led by reason has sometimes to do by the commonwealth's order what he knows to be repugnant to reason, that harm is far compensated by the good which he derives from the civil state."[18] This sort of statement must be seen within the broad acceptance of the "ancient tradition" according to which it is the state's task "to secure for human beings a happier, richer, and safer life," and hence that state and individual are not antagonistic. Rather the state is the product of reason.

Are there then no limits to the security demands of the state? Certainly there are. The importance of freedom of thought and of speech impose such limits. We must now more fully consider the problems which these essential freedoms raise. As we have seen, according to Spinoza man does not

[18] This doctrine, incidentally, is part of Christian teaching of long standing, cf., e.g., Thomas Aquinas, *Summa Theologica* II, I, Q. 96, 4.

surrender his natural rights, when entering the civil state, as he does according to Hobbes, the absolutist (though at one point Spinoza would seem to say so, in the case of democracy). Rather, "the natural right of every man does not cease in the civil state." For man in both states "acts according to the laws of his own nature, and consults his own interest." This statement must be considered in light of Spinoza's radical position, already noted, that agreements, contracts, pledges "remain so long valid as the will of him that gave his word remains unchanged."[19] For this reason, "such things as no one can be induced to do by rewards or threats do not fall within the rights of the commonwealth." Matters of conviction are of this order. You cannot make people believe what is contrary to their convictions; external rights, yes, but faith, no. For this reason, a state which obstructs freedom of thought causes its own ruin. Reason of state, therefore, itself most imperiously demands that freedom of thought be respected, and as a consequence freedom of speech is secured. Spinoza tells us that it was to prove this proposition that he composed the *Theologico-Political Treatise* which he concludes with a vigorous vindication of this freedom.[20] "No one can abdicate his freedom of judgment and feeling . . . men thinking in diverse and contradictory fashions cannot, without disastrous results, be compelled to speak only according to the dictates of the supreme power." Yet, Spinoza would readily impose limits upon the freedom of speech: "its unlimited concession would be most baneful," he says. What is the ultimate aim of government, he asks once more. Not to rule, but to free every man from fear. To put it another way, the purpose of government is not to change men

[19] *Pol. Tr.,* II, 12. Cf. also *Theol.-Pol. Tr.,* ch. XVI, and *Pol. Tr.,* III, 14 on the breaking of treaties.
[20] *Theol.-Pol. Tr.,* ch. XVII and XX; E. I, 214 ff, and 257 ff.

from rational beings into beasts or puppets, but to enable them to develop their minds as well as their bodies. "The true aim of government is liberty."

Freedom of speech depends, in the last analysis, upon what are the intentions of the speaker. Though not giving a "clear and present danger" doctrine, Spinoza's thought tends in that direction.

Supposing a man shows that a law is repugnant to sound reason and should therefore be repealed; if he submits his opinion to the judgment of the authorities . . . and meanwhile acts in accordance with that law, he has deserved well of the state, and has behaved as a good citizen should; but if he accuses the authorities of injustice, and stirs up the people against them, or if he seditiously strives to abrogate the law without their consent, he is a mere agitator and rebel.

Evidently, Spinoza would condemn any speech that was "subversive"; if what a man says disturbs the public peace it cannot be defended under that basic freedom. And yet, Spinoza feels somehow ill at ease in this position. He would, as he proceeds in the argument, rather stress the "action" someone takes than his "opinion." Admittedly, there are opinions which are "seditious" "from the deeds which they involve," but evidently the government should go easy. "If we hold to the principle that a man's loyalty to the state should be judged, like his loyalty to God, from his actions only . . . we cannot doubt that the best government will allow freedom of philosophic speculation no less than of religious belief." Free thought should be granted, because it is a virtue, and free speech because it helps to develop this virtue. He who tries to regulate everything by law merely arouses resistance. What is worse, the effort to shackle freedom of thought and speech arouses the best men, as it makes them think that it is not shameful but honorable to stir up seditions. Such an effort at inhibiting freedom of thought, therefore, stirs the upright into opposing the government; it cannot be maintained without great peril to the state! "He who knows himself to be upright does not fear the death of a criminal, and shrinks from no punishment," Spinoza very poignantly remarks. "Death for freedom is glory," he adds, and the history of our time amply illustrates the wisdom of this reasoning.

Although Spinoza nowhere introduces the actual term "reason of state" in this discussion, it is very clear that "it is imperative that freedom of judgment be granted," if authority is to be maintained and the government is to avoid "yielding to agitators." More especially in a democracy, "everyone submits to the control of authority over his actions, but not over his judgment and reason . . . the voice of the majority has the force of law, subject to repeal, if circumstances bring about a change of opinion." Spinoza adduces the example of Amsterdam in his day to prove his contention that freedom of thought and speech enhance the security of a state, and contrasts it sharply with the former religious intolerance of Remonstrants and Counterremonstrants. "From all these considerations it is clearer than the sun at noon that the true schismatics are those who condemn other men's writings, and seditiously stir up the quarrelsome masses against their authors. . . . In fact, the real disturbers of the peace are those who, in a free state, seek to curtail the liberty of judgment which they are unable to tryannize over." Summing up his arguments, Spinoza concludes that this freedom is "even necessary for the preservation" of the government. "The safest way for a *civitas* (and *a fortiori* for a democratic one) is . . . that every man should think what he likes and say what he thinks." It is clear that Spinoza would insist that in this one vital field of constitutional liberty the maintenance of freedom is the true constitutional reason of state. For the rest, the problem of reason of state is for Spinoza, as for Machiavelli, of quite limited importance. Freedom of thought and speech apart, he thinks only in terms of the absolute forms in which power is concentrated in the hands of one, of a few or of all; reason of state is whatever the rulers deem necessary for security and survival. But Spinoza's ground is different from that of Machiavelli. Reason being the basis of both the constitutional order and its law, there can be no real "reason" for the citizens of a state (and more especially a democratic one) to object to whatever has been determined by law to be necessary for its security and survival.

Another thinker of great importance in the history of constitutionalism is Montesquieu (1689-1755). The very center of his interest being the contrast between constitutional and tyrannical or rather despotic government, Montesquieu might be expected to display a particular concern with the problem of security and survival. Such is indeed the case. His preoccupation with the fate of Republican Rome—why did it fall?—is only one facet of this abiding interest.[21] Montesquieu, too, praises Machiavelli as a key thinker[22] and while correcting

[21] For Montesquieu consult especially A. Sorel, *Montesquieu* (1887), somewhat over-rated, and published prior to the great edition of Montesquieu's works by the great specialist and editor of the works; Henry Barckhausen, *Montesquieu* (1907) and *Montesquieu's Esprit des Lois et les Archives de la Brède* (1904); Joseph Dedieu, *Montesquieu et la Tradition Politique Anglaise en France* (1909); P. Barrière, *Un Grand Provincial: Charles-Louis Secondat, Baron de la Brède et de Montesquieu* (1946) and the memorial volume, issued by the Institut de Droit Comparé, entitled *La Pensée Politique et Constitutionelle de Montesquieu, Bicentenaire de L'Esprit des Lois, 1748-1948* (1952), and the special issue of *Revue Internationale de Philosophie,* Fasc. 3-4 (1955) containing articles by Chevallier, Hendel, Derathé and Cotta (among others), as well as a supplement to D. C. Cabeen's *Montesquieu: a Bibliography* (1947—annotated).

[22] See E. Levi-Malvano, *Montesquieu e Machiavelli* (1912) on whom

Victor Klemperer built his analysis in his *Montesquieu* (1914-5); Cf. him, follows him in his pre-occupation with making freedom and constitutional government (the republic) secure.[23] But unlike Machiavelli, Montesquieu had a more limited sense of what Saint Beuve called "the primitive cupidity of human nature."[24] Yet he knew and dreaded the ever-present danger of the abuse of power and the consequent danger of internal subversion of a constitutional regime. In order to cope with it, such a regime needs effective government and an ability to adapt itself to new situations. Such effective government presupposes vigorous participation of local and corporate entities, the intermediary powers, as Montesquieu called them. In a significant transformation of Locke's doctrine, he expanded

---

especially I, 171, and II, 269. In the latter passage he comments upon book XXVI of the *Spirit of the Laws* as follows: "Perhaps nowhere has Montesquieu had an equally strong sense of combatting Machiavellianism; certainly he is nowhere more Machiavellian than here." Cf. also the striking contrast drawn by Saint-Beuve, *Portraits of the Eighteenth Century* (tr. K. P. Wormley) pp. 107-156, especially p. 138ff. An interesting, somewhat more specialized treatment is Marc Duconseil, *Machiavel et Montesquieu—Recherche sur un Principe d'Autorité* (1943). The range of Italian influence is discussed in Enrico Vidal, *Saggio sul Montesquieu . . .* (1950) ch. IV with rich bibliographical notes.

[23] I am omitting the problem of whether Montesquieu favors monarchical or republican government; I believe he was rather indifferent, provided either is "constitutional," and the nobility given an effective role.

[24] Saint-Beuve stresses the point a bit too much. His general observation that Montesquieu "reasoned upon history" is very well taken, though. I should like to recall the great Gibbon's enthusiastic comment: "I read Grotius and Pufendorf; I read Barbeyrac; I read Locke and his Treatises; but my delight is to read and re-read Montesquieu, whose vigor of style and boldness of hypothesis are so potent to rouse and stimulate the genius of the age." Roger B. Oake, "Montesquieu's Analysis of Roman History" in *Journal of Ideas, XVI* (1955), pp. 44-59 argues effectively against Barckhausen and Laboulaye that Montesquieu considered Rome's militarism and imperialism the effective cause of her decadence as a republic.

the federative power to cover internal as well as external security, and renamed it the executive power whose primary task thus becomes security. He knew and yet he feared the device of constitutional dictatorship. There is a little known tract of his, setting forth an imaginary conversation between Sylla, the Roman dictator, and Eukrates, his friend. Sylla defends his actions as ultimately calculated to restore liberty— and says that is the reason he has resigned his power and submitted his actions to the Roman people to judge, claiming that they were necessary emergency actions. But Eukrates answers him: "In taking over the dictatorship, you have given an example of the crime which you have punished. Here is an example that will be followed, and not that of a moderation which one can only admire. When the Gods suffered Sylla to make himself dictator in Rome, they banished liberty for ever."[25] The point here is that Sylla in his fury had already done so many things to undermine Roman virtue that his return of the power to the people (because he did not wish to rule over slaves) was an empty gesture. In his *Grandeur et Décadence des Romains,* ch. XI, Montesquieu observes similarly that the "fantasie" which made Sylla quit the dictatorship "seemed to give life back to the republic," but that Sylla had actually, "in the furor of his success," done things which made it "impossible for Rome to conserve her liberty." In an earlier chapter (VIII) Montesquieu contrasts Britain with Rome and Carthage as "wise," because she has arranged for a corps (parliament) which continually examines both the government and itself, and thereby stops errors, before they become too

[25] One might note in passing that a similar reproach was often made to Chancellor Brüning by his critics. Cf. F. M. Watkins, *The Failure of Constitutional Emergency Powers under the German Republic* (1939).

serious. To this, he adds the more general principle that "in a word, a free government, that is to say one which is continually in motion (agité) cannot maintain itself, if it is not capable of correcting itself by its proper laws." Although it may seem trite now, this statement contains in fact a major discovery. Montesquieu had a real sense of the rigidity and static quality of a "government by laws." He realized that law and more particularly a basic law can be a straightjacket.[26] He therefore made this power to amend even the most basic law a crucial test of the capacity for survival of a given constitutional order. The importance of an amending power (and of an additional emergency power, in case of urgency) was not well understood during either the British or the French revolution. The American constitution is the first which really faced the problem of the amending power clearly, and from this standpoint one might even say that Art. V of the American constitution is the most original part of the constitution. It followed Montesquieu, as in so many things, so in this also that it neglected the constitutional emergency which creates the problem of constitutional dictatorship. Montesquieu had derived from history the lesson that such dictatorship is very dangerous, and he apparently hoped that the organizing of the constituent forces in society, in the form of an amending power, would take care of the problem.

Beyond this, Montesquieu believed that the only solution of the security problem for a republican system, whether aristocratic or democratic, lay in the direction of organizing a "federative" system. For in such a federal union the advantages of a small republic which can handle internal security, but

---

[26] This point, as such, is of course not new. Harrington makes the point several times, e.g. *A System of Politics,* VIII, 14. Cf. also Thomas Aquinas, *Summa Theologica,* II, I. Q. 96, 6.

not external security, are combined with those of a large republic where the reverse is the case.[27] Anticipating the experience of the United States with Huey Long (as well as others before him) Montesquieu wrote:

He who wishes to usurp (power) cannot achieve equal standing in all the federated states. If he becomes too strong in one, he alarms the others; if he subjects a part, that which remains free can resist. . . . If a sedition occurs in one of the member states, the others can pacify it. If some abuses start in one part, they are corrected by the healthy parts. . . ."

Montesquieu adduced the Netherlands and Switzerland in support of these contentions, which have been so largely born out by the experience of the United States since that time. The recent decision of the Supreme Court, ruling that federal sedition and security legislation had superseded and obviated state activity in this field[28] reinforces these arguments. Here again Montesquieu, by seeking to insure security through structuring the constitutional order in such a way as to minimize the dangers, apparently hopes to avoid the need of any sort of special emergency powers.

Is it going too far to surmise that Montesquieu in the very title of his great *Esprit des Lois* wished to combat the "reason of state" reasoning of the absolutists who would make France into a despotic kingdom? Could Montesquieu forget that it was the Richelieus and the Colberts who had most readily talked of "reason of state"? Certainly, he had every reason to be suspicious of the term. And yet, his very realism obliged him to face the issue of security and survival.

[27] See Book IX of the *Esprit des Lois*. The first chapter of this book, dealing with defense, is entitled "Comment les républiques pourvoient à leur sureté."
[28] *Commonwealth of Pa.* v. *Nelson,* 76 Supreme Court 477 (1956).

In conclusion, we may ask what issues were clarified in the political thought of Harrington, Spinoza and Montesquieu as far as the security and survival of a constitutional order are concerned. To what extent and in what way did they forward the solution of the problem of security and survival of such an order, that is to say, of constitutional reason of state? To put it quite baldly, they certainly did not "solve" the problem. But each of these thinkers made an interesting and important contribution to its solution. Harrington clearly perceived the need of an *institutional* safeguard, a special power to deal with the security problems outside the regular channels of constitutional procedure. He also fairly well understood,—basing his arguments mostly on the Roman and Venetian precedent, though misconceiving them in fact,—that such a special power must be strictly limited to the task of restoring the constitution, of dealing with subversion, that it must not be self-appointed and that it ought to be collegial, that is to say, a board rather than an individual. The contribution of Spinoza is of a very different sort. Oblivious to Harrington's organizational concerns, he develops the important distinction between subversive acts and subversive opinions, shows why the latter ought to be allowed as far as possible, and indeed insists that this basic freedom of thought and speech is essential to the security and survival of the political order. Finally, Montesquieu, profoundly troubled by the potential abuse of any institutional safeguard, because of the inclination of men to abuse the power at their disposal, stressed the importance of a flexible constitutional framework. He believed that the constituent power of the people should be organized into an effective amending power through which a constitutional order could be adapted to a changing environment. But on the whole,

Montesquieu was fairly pessimistic; he did not think that there existed a true remedy for the internal corruption of a republic, unless it be the organizing of a federal system.

All in all, these three authors, though definitely aware of the security problems of constitutional reason of state, do not stress sufficiently the subversion of the internal order. All three thought in terms of consolidated national states whose problems of security were those of defense against foreign aggression of a military kind and against the seditious designs of internal opponents of the regime. All three also were believers in aristocratic government and in the beneficial role of the elite, though all three would likewise allow the people at large some share in the making of the basic decisions. The Roman model was a powerful precedent in their thought, reinforced by what at least Harrington and Spinoza believed to have been the characteristics of the commonwealth of ancient Israel. In some important respects, Calvin and the Calvinists, confronted by the tasks of the religious wars, had a more poignant sense of the dangers and potentialities of subversion in its present-day meaning, that is to say, in a situation where a subversive belief system is being supported and promoted by a foreign power. To their thought on constitutional reason of state we now turn.

IV   The Christian Slant

Calvin, the Calvinists and Althusius

THE REFORMERS, DETERMINED to bring the church back to its pristine concern with man's spiritual welfare and to "depoliticize" it radically, were much perplexed by the role to be assigned to the government. Their close attention to Holy Script, as exemplified in the doctrine of the Word, confronted them with the unmistakable acceptance of secular authority by Jesus and Paul. The commentary of Luther and Calvin on Romans XIII bears very clear witness to this central fact. Yet both Calvin and Luther also recognized the role of estates assemblies (and their presumed precedent in Rome) and not only allowed, but claimed for them a decisive share in shaping governmental conduct, at least by restricting the abuse of power by the prince.[1] This conventional authoritarianism produced an image of Christian statesmanship which as stated so far might have left things pretty much as they had been. But their intrinsically revolutionary position, when combined with the doctrine that it is the task of such Christian statesmanship to do all in its power to assist in the maintenance and spread

[1] Cf. Kurt Wolzendorf, *Staatsrecht und Naturrecht in der Lehre vom Widerstandsrecht des Volkes.* (1916).

of the true faith,—a doctrine as old as St. Augustine,—gave these ideas a twist which led to a novel conception of *ratio status*. For reason of state now became sanctified by purposes believed to be transcendental in scope. This is not as far a cry from Machiavelli as might at first appear. For it was to the corrupt popes of his time and the immoral state of the church that Machiavelli had objected, and not to the Christian religion as such. Here, certainly, is a link between the pagan Florentine and the religious reformers of the North. The matter has been obscured by the moral, and more especially Christian indignation which other aspects of Machiavelli's thought have aroused. But as one recent commentator puts it quite well: "What should have been Machiavelli's attitude to the diabolical policy of Julius the second?"[2] This solution of the problem which such corruption posited was, however, radically at variance with Machiavelli's. For Machiavelli asked for a return to the political thought of classical antiquity which made the state the respository of all value, and hence he pinned his hope upon the arrival of a great legislator and statebuilder, a philosopher king in the Platonic tradition who would purge and unite Italy and presumably force the church to forgo its secular pretensions and to purify its spiritual undertaking by concentrating upon religion. Luther, on the other hand, demanded a return to early Christian faith, and to the community of the saints. He viewed the political order as not of decisive importance, as devoid of primary value and hence as something to be accepted and to be submitted to by the true Christian.

Thus Luther like Machiavelli could not really see the problem of reason of state in its full dialectic. For Luther all politics was bad, in the Christian perspective, and hence its prob-

[2] Whitfield, op. cit. Cf. also the famous ch. XV in Bk I of the *Discourses* for all this.

lems could only be handled by men who acknowledged their depravity and sinfulness and made the best of a bad bargain. The state, devoid of true justice, is fully and inexorably involved in man's depravity. Yet, there is found in Luther a line of thought which could, and in the Calvinist version does, open up an approach to politics that rationalizes the means which the necessities of the situation require. Luther stresses the doctrine of vocation or calling. This doctrine is embedded in older Christian orthodoxy. But it acquires a new emphasis in Luther and through Luther, because of the sanctification of all manner of work. To put it dramatically, work is the test of faith. This doctrine of work he juxtaposes to the doctrine of justification through works. In one of his early sermons he therefore wrote:

I fulfill the commands of the Lord when I teach and pray, the plowman when he listens and does his farm work diligently; and the prince and his officials do not fulfill them, when they cannot be found when needed, but say that they must pray—for that means to withdraw from God's true service in the name of God.

The Protestant doctrine of the calling found perhaps its most pointed expression in Luther's *Whether Soldiers may be in a blessed state?* which, while admitting a limited pacifism, in case the war is unjust, urges the right to fight in a defensive war and then to do all that is necessary. The same holds true, of course, and more strongly, for the prince and his officials. It also applies, *ceteris paribus,* to the citizen who is, after all, especially in a constitutional democracy, in fact a civilian soldier. All these must do what is necessary in the circumstances of political life, they must live up to the requirements of their respective vocations in the commonwealth. Calvin and his followers developed the doctrine of the calling more fully than anyone before them. The position of Luther on the calling is by the Calvinists gradually expanded into a central doctrine of the Protestant faith. It is the counter-weight to the doctrine of predestination. The harsh idea that God in His infinite wisdom has elected some men for eternal salvation, while many others are damned could not but produce a feeling of despair in the minds of those who firmly believed it. There can be no question that this feeling was very strong in Luther. But he sought and found release in the strength of his religious faith. So did Calvin and others after him. But for many more ordinary men, less capable of religious thought and emotion, a great void was created by the frightfulness of an inescapable damnation. And since there was nothing man could do, by works or deeds, to affect the divine decision, it became a question of desperate concern by what signs one might know whether one belonged or not. Strictly speaking, no signs were certain. But gradually, the idea gained ground that success in one's wordly calling was a sign of probability, that it opened the gate of some hope, no matter how vague. Add to this the purely psychological escape from anxiety which work provides for most men, and the extraordinary intensity of inner-worldly activity characteristic of Calvinists is made comprehensible.

It is well-known that Max Weber made this aspect of Protestant teachings the basis of his brilliant *Protestant Ethic and the Spirit of Capitalism*. His thesis was that the increasing emphasis upon effective rationalization of all business activity which produced capitalism grew directly out of the doctrine of man's calling or vocation which Calvinism developed. His pointed theme has been subjected to detailed criticism by a whole host of writers who have tried to show that capitalism started long before Protestantism, that it grew from other roots than religious conviction and moral ideas, that Protestantism was anti-capitalist and so forth.[3] Some of these criticisms were

[3] See Max Weber, *The Protestant Ethic and the Spirit of Capitalism*

well-taken, others missed the point of Weber's analysis. To impute to capitalism a "spirit" was, to many, a very unfortunate attempt to confuse the basic economic issues involved. But the fact of the matter is that Weber's thesis has remained a highly significant, if perhaps somewhat overstated insight.[4] Yet in most discussions of Weber's thesis its central weakness has been overlooked. This weakness results from Weber's preoccupation with the economic, as contrasted with the governmental sphere. At least some of the difficulties with his thesis which have provided ammunition to his critics are traceable to the fact that there is an interval between the emergence of the Protestant doctrine of calling and the crystallization of an outlook which might be called "spirit of capitalism." During this interval, the tendency toward rationalizing inner-worldly activity first took hold of government and the state, and spread from there to the economic sphere.

It is no accident that Luther in the passage we cited confronts the preacher with the prince, reinforcing his argument with the peasant who plows his field. The plowman is a traditional figure and there is no suggestion here of any "ration-

---

(ed. Talcott Parsons, 1930), R. H. Tawney, *Religion and the Rise of Capitalism* (1926), Amintore Fanfani, *Catholicism, Protestantism and Capitalism* (1935), E. Troettsch, *Die Bedeutung des Protestantismus für die Entstehung der Modernen Welt* (1911—Engl. tr. *Protestantism and Progress,* 1930), H. M. Robertson, *The Rise of Economic Individualism* (1933), J. B. Kraus, *Scholastik, Puritanismus und Kapitalismus* (1930). Weber's original study was published in 1904/5 in the *Archiv für Sozialwissenschaft und Sozialphilosophie.* That Weber draws much of his illustrative material concerning the ethics of Protestantism from so late a Calvinist as Baxter (1615-1691) has often been remarked by critics.

[4] See Talcott Parsons' Introduction to his English translation of Weber's work, taking issue with Tawney's study, and the same author's summary of his Heidelberg dissertation, "Capitalism in Recent German Literature: Sombart and Weber" 2. instalment, *The Journal of Political Economy,* XXXVII, 31ff.

alization." But that the prince who fails to be available for needed work, because he must pray, is neglecting God's work, is a novel note. To be sure, in the notion that governmental activity must be seen as part of the divine scheme of things, there is no break between Luther and Thomas Aquinas such as has often been suggested. For both, the calling or vocation of government has a divine purpose and meaning. But whereas for Aquinas and his age the most exalted calling was that of the monk who dedicates his life to the specific service of Christ, for Luther the monk's is no calling at all, no true vocation; all genuine "callings" are responded to in this world. It has been said that Luther was of the opinion that God is felt as reality in the full sense only by him who takes upon himself life in its full exigency, with all its disappointments and tensions.[5] These notions had already turned up among the mystics, men like Master Eckhart and Tauler, but without the radical attack upon the monkish order; in fact they both fully supported and maintained monastic life.

These callings which in Luther's mind tended to be more or less equivalent, as one quotation showed, were by Calvin arranged in a definite hierarchy. Such an hierarchical ordering of man's activities was, of course, not new. It is a recurrent theme in the Middle Ages. Thus Berthold von Regensburg described mankind as divided into ten choirs of which the three highest ones were priests, monks and judges (including lords and knights); into the tenth choir were placed the dishonorable professions, such as usurers, musicians, whores and armament makers. Calvin did not really alter this scheme,

[5] Karl Holl, *Gesammelte Aufsaetze*, III, 189-219, "Die Geschichte des Wortes Beruf,"—a somewhat one-sided presentation which was corrected, from a Catholic standpoint, by Nikolaus Paulus in *Historisches Jahrbuch der Görresgesellschaft*, XLV, pp. 308ff. (1925).

except for the elimination of monks. Priests and judges, church and government service are the highest professions, with the place of the monks taken by the universities. For our present purpose, it is important to notice the high place assigned to the government. For evidently the concept of calling or vocation applies very especially to the government service. Since a vocation calls for vigorous pursuit of the craftsman's kind of success, the man engaged in government is obviously going to be faced with the problems of power, of security and survival and hence will have to act in accordance with the "laws of power," the "necessities" in the Machiavellian sense.

Calvin injected, moreover, a basic complication which raised the problem of reason of state in a new form. Like the most papal of medieval clericalists, Calvin maintained that the clergy must predominate in the state. In the *Institutes of the Christian Religion* (IV, XX, 2) he baldly stated: "It is the purpose of temporal rule, so long as we live among men, to foster and support the external worship of God, to defend pure doctrine and the standing of the church." Therefore his reason of state is at the same time a "reason of church," that is to say, not only the survival and security of the state are a matter of successfully manipulating the "laws of power," but the survival and security of the church as well.[6] What this doctrine implied, politically, was a rigid authoritarianism, including thought control of a thorough fashion in states where the rulers are Calvinists, and a revolutionary radicalism and resistance in non-Calvinist states. The latter implication was only very reluctantly admitted by Calvin himself, but soon manifested itself in numerous writings such as *Vindiciae contra*

---

[6] This view has been challenged by François Wendel, *Calvin, Sources et Evolution de sa Pensée Religieuse* (1950). I am not convinced by his argument.

Tyrannos,[7] Buchanan,[8] and François Hotman.[9] To this literature should be added *De Jure Magistratuum*[10] attributed to
Calvin's successor Theodore Beza, but the evidence is scanty
and inconclusive.

This entire resistance literature was eventually dubbed
*"monarcho*machical" by the monarchist and absolutist William
Barclay in his *De Rege et Regali Potestate* (1600), though its
true import was, of course, *"tyranno*machical," that is to say
calling for the killing of tyrants. It was systematized and provided with a philosophical underpinning by Johannes Althusius, who in 1603 published his *Politica Methodice Digesta,*
of which more elaborate editions followed in 1610 and later.[11]

[7] The *Vindiciae contra Tyrannos* were published under the pseu-
donym Stephanus Junius Brutus in 1579; an English translation appeared in 1648 and often thereafter; it was reprinted in 1924 with an
interesting introduction by Harold Laski. The tract was formerly attributed to Hubert Languet, but was claimed by Max Lossen (*Bayer-
ische Akademie der Wissenschaften,* 1887) for Philippe du Plessis-
Mornay. Waddington, Elkan and Laski followed him, but the most
convincing case has been made out for dual authorship by Isselstyn,
who argues that the third answer and part of the preface are Languet's,
the rest du Plessis-Mornay's; see "L'Auteur de l'Ouvrage Vindiciae
Contra Tyrannos Publié sous le Nom de Stephanus Junius Brutus" in
Revue Historique (1931) with which compare Ernest Barker's discussion in "The Authorship of the *Vindiciae contra Tyrannos*" in *Cambridge Historical Journal,* III, 164ff. (1930).

[8] George Buchanan, *De Jure Regni Apud Scotos* (1578).

[9] François Hotman, *Franco-Gallia* (1573), and the study by Beatrice
Reynolds, *Proponents of Limited Monarchy in Sixteenth Century
France: Francis Hotman and Jean Bodin* (1931).

[10] *De Jure Magistratuum* (anonymous, 1578—Pierre Mesnard speaks
of a French edition of 1575, but gives no detail).

[11] See my *Politica Methodice Digesta of Johannes Althusius (Althaus)*
(1932) which contains an introduction giving an analysis of some key
concepts, as well as such biographical detail as I was able to discover
in the documents. My interpretation somewhat diverges from Otto von
Gierke's well-known treatment in his *Johannes Althusius und die Ent-
wicklung der Naturrechtlichen Staatstheorien* (4. ed., 1929) of which an
English edition by B. Freyd appeared in 1938. There is an interesting

This remarkable work is the most fully developed system of
political theory we have by an orthodox Calvinist. It is noteworthy also for the author's readiness to accept the challenge
of Jean Bodin, who in his *Six Livres de la Republique* or *De
Republica Libri Sex* (1576)[12] had developed the concept of
sovereignty as supreme power of and in the state and had
claimed such sovereignty to be an essential ingredient of any
well-ordered state. But Althusius, in accepting this idea of
sovereignty, at once vindicated it for the politically organized
community as a whole, and called it its inalienable possession.
In order to make this proposition viable, he proceeded to
interpret the politically organized community as a pluralistic
hierarchy of federations, held together on each level by the
bond of living together and sharing possessions, needs and

chapter on Althusius in Pierre Mesnard, *L'Essor de la Philosophie
Politique du Seizième Siècle* (1936) who also deals with some of the
other writers. Erik Wolf has treated Althusius in a chapter of his
Deutsche Rechtsdenker (1939, 2. ed. 1944), vol. I, pp. 167-199. More
recently, a dissertation on Althusius was presented at Yale University
by Stanley J. Parry which it was the author's privilege to read; it is
critical of both Gierke and myself. While much interested, I remain
unconvinced. The practical politics of Althusius has been more fully
explored by H. Antholz in a study entitled "Die Politische Wirksamkeit
des Johannes Althusius in Emden" (1955), *Abhandlungen und Vor-
traege zur Geschichte Ostfrieslands,* Heft XXXII.
[12] Besides Mesnard's excellent treatment in the work just cited, R.
Chauviré's *Jean Bodin, Auteur de la Republique* (1914) and Henri
Baudrillart's *Jean Bodin et Son Temps* (1853) deserve mention; John
Brown's study of the *Methodus ad Facilem Historiarum Cognitionem*
(1566) entitled *The Methodus . . . , A Critical Study* (1939) opened up
significant perspectives. For this and other earlier works of Bodin
Pierre Mesnard's magistral edition in *Corpus Général des Philosophes
Français,* Vol. V, 3 "Jean Bodin" (1951) should now be standard. The
Harvard University Press will soon publish the English edition of
Bodin's book on the state, made by Knowles in 1606, with an introduction by Kenneth MacRae who also recently completed an excellent
dissertation on *Bodin's Political Theory* at Harvard which will, it is
hoped, be published also.

interests, as well as cherishing common ends. This bond he saw as resting upon *symbiosis,* and hence the state as well as the hierarchally ordered groups are seen as symbiotic associations. The natural symbiotic group being the family, the heads of families then form guilds, or villages, the guilds a town, the villages a country district, the towns and districts a county, the counties a province, the provinces a kingdom or state. Throughout the tiers, government is organized cooperatively (to call it democratic would be misleading) upon the basis of agreements or *foedera.*

It is within this context of a cooperative associational order, a federative constitutional system, that Althusius' doctrine of a reason of state must be seen and analyzed. For Althusius, as for many others, especially those interested in the scientific revolution, reason and nature are linked to one another as concomitant explanatory principles. The *ratio* or reason of a thing is no longer primarily its end or purpose,[13] but its mode of operation. To understand the *ratio* of something requires an understanding of the laws it is subject to. Richard Hooker, in his *Laws of Ecclesiastical Polity* (I, VIII, 4), gives a general definition of law which fits this prevailing outlook well. "A law," he writes, "therefore generally taken, is a directive rule unto goodness of operation." In voluntary agents, it is "the sentence that Reason giveth." Thus *ratio* refers to general laws or principles, as well as to the particular requirements of a living individual. Such a living individual may be a single human being, a family, a guild, a city or finally a state. All these groups have their own general *rationes,* as well as the particular *ratio* of this particular individual, group or state. These natural requirements, whether general or particular,

---

[13] See for a discussion of this problem my introduction to *Johannes Althusius Politica Methodice Digesta* (1932), pp. LXXV ff.

can be realized only by actions rationally adapted to their ends. Thus each of these *rationes* is compounded of those general principles which are true for all human beings, all families, all guilds, all churches, all cities and all states, and of the particular needs and requirements of each particular being. The word *ratio* applies to both these aspects, and it is inadmissible to construct an antithesis between a generalizing *ratio status,* prevalent in the sixteenth century, and an individualizing one which predominates later.[14] The interest in sound generalization does not prevent Althusius any more than Machiavelli from recognizing individual requirements.

Althusius often uses the expression *ratio administrationis* instead of *ratio status.* This *ratio* is compounded of the general principles of good government and an understanding of the particular necessities of a particular association. In either case, it rests upon knowledge, i.e., political prudence which consists of two elements: knowing the ends of political association and understanding what means will produce the desired results.[15] It is evident that Althusius' discussion of this *ratio administrationis* bears a close resemblance to Bodin's *ratio gubernandi.* He goes, however, considerably further than Bodin in accepting the Machiavellian notion of political necessity.

We must take Althusius' doctrine of reason of state very seriously, for in his frame of reference, which is the constitutionally organized political community, reason of state presents problems which do not exist for Machiavelli or even Bodin. For as we have seen, only those political theorists who subject government and politics to law and/or a transcendent

[14] This was done by Friedrich Meinecke, op. cit., pp. 431 and elsewhere.
[15] See *Politica* XXI, 6-16, 25, and 59 ff.

moral order, who put justice ahead of or at least on a level with peace and order are confronted with the problem of reason of state in its most perplexing form. For if the constitutional order's survival is threatened by an enemy who does not acknowledge the validity of this law and moral order, what is the defender of the constitutional order permitted to do? How far may he go in violating the norms which he is supposedly bound to respect? This is not merely or simply the question of moral conduct of the individual involved in the situation; it may well raise the issue with reference to the conduct of the constitutionally organized community itself.

The test case is, of course, the problem of treaty observance which Machiavelli had put simply in terms of a dependence upon a continuing interest in the maintenance of the treaty (*clausula rebus sic stantibus*). It is very revealing that Althusius is prepared to go almost as far as Machiavelli in this field, as indeed were Harrington and Spinoza (see pp. 34 ff.). His discussion of the policy of alliances varies little from that of Machiavelli's followers.[16] Similarly, Althusius accepts the violations of the moral code which occur during wartime in the conduct of governmental affairs.[17] In view of this attitude it is not surprising that Althusius goes a long way in approving the very methods which today are so highly controversial in constitutional states in connection with the maintenance of public order and security. He explicitly includes among the techniques to be employed the use of informers, of spies and tortures for the discovery of seditions. In seeking to prove his

[16] See *Politica,* XXXIV, 49-51.
[17] See Op. cit., XXXV, 57 and elsewhere. Althusius' phrasing is very broad: "Insidiae, igitur, stratagemata, astutia, solertia and dolus in bello contra hostem sunt licita," he writes, and cites Machiavelli's *Discorsi* (giving it the title *De Republica*) III, 14, as well as Botero and Lipsius.

point, Althusius makes recurrent reference to Botero and Lipsius, both in the absolutist tradition of reason of state. Like these writers, he advises the government, when confronted with a rebellion and the task of overcoming it, to give vague promises at first, in order to gain the upper hand, and then to proceed to the forcible suppression of the rebellious elements. In keeping with his general inclination of drawing upon the Bible for political and social experience, as well as for value judgments, Althusius repeatedly refers to the rebellion of Absalom for the discovery of which King David used a spy.[18] It has recently been shown that "in any case, his political practice and his skillful legal casuistry in adapting himself to the necessities of the moment is not far removed from the world of Machiavelli."[19] All in all, it would appear to be his view that the defenders of a constitutional order are justified in doing whatever the situation requires.

But he provides a very different underpinning for this view than Machiavelli. Having constructed the community in terms of a mutual give and take of sympathy, affection and charity, that is to say, upon a broad base of sociability going well beyond that assumed by Aristotle and other ancients, these acts flow from the government's recognition of what it owes the community for which it speaks. Not the search for power, but the practice of good will causes the government to act with sole regard to the *ratio* of the community's interests and needs. The ruthlessness which may be implicit in such actions is veiled in the cloak of a protective duty.

[18] See II *Sam.* 15, 34ff. and 17. Cf. also II *Sam.* 2, 6-7; 3, 7-13; 15, 31-32; 19, 23; 20; *Judges* 8, 1ff, *Numbers* 14, 6ff. Some of these events might just as well have been cited by Machiavelli.
[19] Antholz, op. cit., p. 222. He gives a number of examples of this "reason of state" in practice.

It is interesting in this connection to discover that the same rationalizing approach to the use of morally dubious means was applied to the conduct of such inferior magistrates as may find themselves in the position of having to defend the community's legal order against a tyrannical superior. Reason of state is not merely at the disposal of the monarch or other *de facto* ruler, but applies to the conduct of any and all those to whom the constitutional order assigns a part of governmental authority. Althusius consequently also speaks of a *ratio officii* or "reason of office," by which he means the rationalized conduct of any office. Such office must be rationalized in terms of its needs and requirements, and more especially in terms of the "laws of nature" as applicable to that particular sphere of social life.[20] Thus the *ephori* which, for Althusius as for Calvin, are appointed as guardians of the constitution will proceed with such guile as the situation calls for, and obviously they will be obliged to act in accordance with the laws of power. "The law of necessity" to which the parliamentarians appealed during Pride's Purge is part and parcel of this outlook, and Milton's arguments for justifying the execution of King Charles are foreshadowed in Althusius' doctrine of *ratio administrationis*.

The shift from *ratio status* to *ratio administrationis* enabled Althusius to perceive that reason of state is only one specific manifestation of a general principle, the principle that human beings when acting on behalf of groups tend to accept the group's objectives and purposes as beyond discussion. How to realize these ends becomes then a technical problem: how to administer the group efficiently, how to combat both its internal and external enemies with all the skill available, how to broaden the foundation of its security and survival. The

[20] For the *ratio officii* see *Politica*, XXI, 10 and throughout.

68

very fact that Althusius thinks in "biotic," that is to say vital-istic, terms, that the living together is made the pivotal point of his political analysis leads him toward such radical conclusions as these. But in spite of the obvious dangers that thus every-one who wields public authority becomes "Machiavellian" in the defense of his particular share of governmental power, Althusius does not go very far in specifying the legal frame-work for the exercise of such checks and balances, as they later were called. There is prevalent in Althusius' thought a broad confidence in the intrinsic rationality of human beings. This natural rationality is the condition of the common life. From this point of view knowledge has a strictly pragmatic value. It is of great significance in facilitating the successful cooperation among men. The man who knows what is useful to the state, not he who knows much, deserves praise.[21] To be sure, Althusius, like most Calvinists, is preoccupied with the immediately practical and does not realize to what extent such preoccupation with immediate utility interferes with thorough scientific inquiry; like Machiavelli, he has the temper of an engineer rather than of a scientist. If one thinks, so the argu-ment runs, he does it in order to act more effectively; sciences are founded upon their utility.[22]

The great role of the *ratio,* then, lies in the fact that it en-ables men to fulfill their function in government and society to the best of their ability. It enables them to mould the con-

[21] See *Politica,* XXI, 12. The same opinion is to be found in Cicero, *De Officiis* I, 19 and 157-8. This instance is only one of many in which the highly rational view of Roman stoicism impinges, in the train of humanist learning, upon Western political thought. For it is after all one of the main sources of inspiration for Machiavelli's outlook.

[22] For further detail on the Calvinist preference for the active life which Althusius completely shares see my Introduction to *Politica,* pp. LXXVIIf. Their outlook is in sharp contrast to Aristotle as well as Bodin.

duct of their respective offices in the light of all the scientific facts and insights that can be gathered. For it broadens their understanding of causal sequences. And since all of social life is God's creation, such rationalization of its various phases contributes to the greater glory of God. Knowledge, even of a very technical sort, is thus vital to realizing God's purpose. This was eventually summed up in many a seventeenth century defense of Machiavelli as follows: as long as the ruler's intentions are right, that is, directed towards Christian ends, he cannot be judged by the ethical value of individual actions.[23] This is, of course, nothing but the doctrine that the end justifies the means. These means are clearly seen as determined by their "instrumental rationality"[24]

It is in this connection that the high value of higher education becomes manifest. Ignorance is the abiding source of trouble and it is only through education that rational conduct can be assured. "The spirit when it enters the body is like a blank sheet," Althusius writes at one point. "Ignorance of all things is inborn into it. Notions must therefore afterwards be written upon it, so that knowledge may follow. . . ."[25] We see here the tap root of that concern with scientific training which gave such powerful impetus to the rationalization of the professional government service. Indeed, the development of modern responsible bureaucracy is unthinkable without it.[26]

[23] See George L. Mosse, in an article on "The Christian Statesman" in *The History of Ideas News Letter* (March 1955), p. 3.

[24] This point is admirable developed for English Calvinists by George L. Mosse in an article entitled "The Assimilation of Machiavelli in English Thought: The Casuistry of William Perkins and William Ames" in *The Huntington Library Quarterly*, XVII (1954), pp. 315-326.

[25] *Oratio Panegyrica, De Necessitate, Utilitate et Antiquitate Scholarum* (1603) printed as an appendix to the *Politica*.

[26] Perhaps the most penetrating analysis of the link between Calvinism and the development of a rationalized bureaucracy was made by

Through such training, a man is placed in the position of understanding better the "will of God" as expressed in laws of nature which provide the matrix for his work. It would be a mistake to assume that this was a wholly novel approach. Thomist rationalism definitely tended in this direction; but due to the mediating role assigned to church authorities in interpreting this will of God, the inherent tendencies toward rationalization in secular and scientific terms were held in check. This check was greatly weakened under the influence of Protestantism, and more especially Calvinism. In no sphere was this more revolutionary than in that of political activities. Obviously, if the decision as between the pressing requirements of a concrete power situation and the higher reason of ethical norms is put up to the conscience of the prince or any other politicians, the doors are opened for the kind of calculation which characterizes the political thought of men like Cromwell and William III. They both would have thoroughly approved of Althusius' emphasis upon the ten commandments as guide posts for the *ratio* which the highest magistrate is to employ in the performance of his various tasks. But they would likewise have agreed that there are many situations,—exceptional situations, to be sure,—in which the needs and requirements will call for exceptions to these rules.

It is fundamentally a question of the degree of latitude which is being allowed, and of the persons to whom such

---

Otto Hintze, "Kalvinismus und Staatsräson in Brandenburg zu Beginn des 17. Jahrhunderts" in *Historische Zeitschrift*, vol. 144, pp. 229-286. Hintze, in this article, revived an earlier position of Droysen, but instead of stressing the role of the prince, Elector Johann Sigismund, he emphasized that of certain key officials, especially von Rheydt, whom he considers the key exponent of the Dutch and French *raison d'Etat;* cf. also the literature cited in my *Constitutional Government and Democracy* (3 ed., 1950) Chapters II, XIX.

discretion is assigned. For Althusius and others of his general outlook the degree of latitude is very narrow, indeed, calling for the utmost caution, circumspection and moderation in all cases of both internal and external security. Rulers should be forever on guard against acting severely, cruelly or impetuously in situations involving factionalism, sedition and the like. Indeed, he keeps reminding his readers that such disturbances often are the fault of the rulers. Partly for this reason, discretion in such matters of state is not restricted to the prince or ruler, but is shared by guardians (*ephori*) who, when there is no chance to restrain the ruler, will act in accordance with necessity (as in war).

This is the point of sharpest conflict with Bodin who would entrust the discretion in such matters entirely to the sovereign. "The prince or the people in whom sovereignty is (vested) are not compelled to render an account of things done to anyone except to the immortal God."[27] In consequence, the citizen, called by Bodin *le franc sujet,* is bound to absolute obedience, except for a limited religious sphere. In this connection, Bodin develops a sharp distinction between the *droit* and the *loi,* and insists that the citizen cannot appeal from the *loi* to the *droit,* from the positive law to the law of nature. For the *droit* belongs to the realm of principle; it does not apply to concrete factual situations except by action of the sovereign prince. Without the latter, it is inoperative. Hence it is both stupid and improper to invoke *droit* against the law: "ce seroit le crime de lèze majesté d'opposer le droit Romain à l'ordonnance de son prince."[28]

Althusius, on the other hand, insists that the *jus* (*droit*) is

---

[27] *De Republica* I, 8; See also III, 4. See also Pierre Mesnard, *L'Essor de la Philosophie Politique au XVIe Siecle* (new ed., 1951) pp. 480-494.
[28] Mesnard, op. cit., p. 492.

all imbedded in the law of the community. Preoccupied as he is with the principles to be derived from the Decalogue, Althusius would not only allow the official to resist deviations from this basic set of commandments, but would suggest that his *ratio officii* makes it his duty to do so. More particularly those guardians of the constitutional order, the ephors who represent the people in estates' assemblies, must be constantly on the alert and ready to employ their power for the purpose of keeping the community's legal order in line with this higher law.[29]

This argument between Bodin and Althusius shows that the idea of sovereignty served both writers to institutionalize the activities which the *ratio status* in the light of the requirements for the security and survival of the state necessitated. But whereas Bodin inclined to the view that the most dependable repository of this ultimate power to defend the legal order was a prince such as the king of France, Althusius claimed that this *ultima ratio* is irrevocably vested in the organized community itself which would express its will-to-live through its duly authorized representatives. The office of such representatives thus becomes a noble calling, indeed, but it remains subordinate to the constituent power of the people which has created the political order.[30] Beyond this ultimate check, it would seem that the authorities are completely in charge of the *ratio status* which is the *ratio administrations* of a well ordered Christian commonwealth.

In short, Althusius, like Calvin, leaves us without any clear indication as to the procedure which might limit the exercise

[29] For all this, see my Introduction to the *Politica*, as cited, pp. XCIV ff.

[30] For this constituent power, see my Introduction, loc. cit., p. LXXXVIII and XCI.

of such emergency powers. "What if the organized community through its representatives should decide to do something which is contrary to the commandments of God, to the supreme command of neighbourly love? This question remains unanswered, but undoubtedly the answer would be: they will never make such a decision, if they are of the true Christian faith. They may do something which is an adaptation of these commandments to the conditions of time, place and so on, but they will never do anything wholly contrary to them, unless in the strictest sense necessary for survival. At this point, we are face to face with the ultimate religious foundation of the political thought of Althusius and the Calvinists. We are confronted with a faith."[31]

That is the reason why, in their way, Calvin and the Calvinists were often such remarkable Machiavellians. Their self-righteous cant prevented them from recognizing any institutional problem at all. They were as "naive" about the problem of the abuse of power by the righteous, as many politicians and writers of the free world today. As William Sancroft put it, in commenting on the practice of Puritan England in 1652: "It does me a little relish of paradox, that wherever I come Machiavelli is verbally cursed and damned, and yet practically embraced and asserted."[32] What Sancroft should have realized is that Protestant ethic and ascetic, in so far as it permeates the state with its powerful sense of service, comes close to the *virtù* ideal of Machiavelli. The maintenance of a vigorous citizenship able to defend and govern the state is the central concern, in both.

---

[31] See Introduction to my *Althusius Politica*, XCVIII.
[32] William Sancroft, *Modern Politics Taken from Machiavel, Borgia and Other Choice Authors, by an Eye Witness* (1652); also cited in Mosse, loc. cit., p. 326.

V   The Moralist Slant

Milton, Locke, Kant

THE INHERENT POLITICAL *rationale* of Calvinist thought which Althusius so clearly grasped, also made itself felt in a number of Puritan writers in England. Gradually their thinking assimilated "reason of state" as they undertook the task of building the Godly commonwealth of the saints, both in old and new England.[1] But their penchant toward constitutionalism which was related to their political as well as their ecclesiastical position, revolving as it did around the issues of church government, soon created for them, or for those who were acute enough to recognize it, the typical problems of *constitutional* reason of state.

Sovereignty interpreted as the constituent power and this constituent power of the people reinforced by an emergency power of its representatives,—such was the solution of Althusius to the problem of security and survival of a constitutional order. But it all hinged upon the confident belief that all men, all citizens would eventually be believing Christians in Calvin's sense. It was essentially the doctrine underlying John Milton's

[1] See for this general trend the fine article by George L. Mosse, "Puritanism and Reason of State in Old and New England" in *William and Mary Quarterly* (1952) pp. 67-80. He points out the importance of the concept of "policy" as a design of such statecraft at the time.

(1608-1674) three works, justifying the revolution and the execution of Charles the King, *The Tenure of Kings and Magistrates* (1648/9), *Eikonoklastes* (1649) and the two Defenses: *Defensio pro Populo Anglicano* (1651) and *Defensio Secunda* (1654). But it was, in Milton, reinforced by an independent reason and deeply affected by his attachment to freedom of speech and thought. These he, like Spinoza, considered essential to a healthy Commonwealth, as especially expounded in his *Areopagitica* (1644). In all these works, Milton treats security and survival of the free commonwealth as calling for the forceful suppression of those who would challenge freedom. "Reason of commonwealth," if such a phrase be allowed, was quite absolute. When the *salus populi* was truly at stake, as was the case in a free commonwealth, restraints could not be allowed to hamper the action of the government. In this sense, he was an uncompromising rationalizer of the revolutionary dictatorship of Cromwell. To him, there seems to have been no problem involved in the question which puzzles us, namely, what to do with people who themselves would not admit freedom of expression. Papists, prelaticals and the like must all be obviously kept out of such a commonwealth.

And yet there seems to have been an equally forceful recognition of the limitations of royal reason of state. *Eikonoklastes* is sprinkled with references suggesting that the king had no right to appeal to such a norm as one justifying his actions. The terms of abuse Milton showers upon Charles Stuart all culminate in the charge that he is a "hypocrite," when offering such pleas. Yet, is not that precisely what Milton's own attitude can be charged with? To him, it is all a matter of the end. Since there is no question about the commonwealth's end being the common weal, its rationale is taken for granted.

Since the king's government is oppression of the people, the opposite holds for him. Here is the very crux, the root of the "crisis," suggesting once more the nature of the issue: reason of state was built upon a self-righteous identification of the government's view with the general interest—reason of commonwealth was no less.

In *Areopagitica* Milton had sensed more definitely the deeper dialectic of the issue, though he does not really come to grips with it. His eloquent plea for liberty of the press and for freedom of expression, celebrated these three hundred years, does not attempt to draw the line between freedom and license:

And though all the winds of doctrine were let loose to play upon the earth, so truth be in the field, we do injuriously by licensing and prohibiting to misdoubt her strength. Let her and falsehood grapple; who ever knew truth put to the worse, in a free and open encounter? Her confuting is the best and surest suppressing." "For who knows not that truth is strong, next to the Almighty; she needs no policies, nor stratagems, nor licensing to make her victorious; those are the shifts and the defences that error uses against her power: give her but room. . . .

The same Milton could, thirty years later, writing *Of True Religion, Heresy, Schism, Toleration* (published 1671), seek to show that "popery, being idolatrous, is not to be tolerated either in public or private." It is a sentiment which was powerful during the Commonwealth, and firmly expressed in the very paragraphs on religious freedom, included in the *Instrument of Government* (1653):

That such as profess faith in God by Jesus Christ . . . shall not be restrained from, but shall be protected in, the profession of the faith and exercise of their religion; . . . provided this liberty be not extended to Popery or Prelacy, nor to such as, under the profession of Christ, hold forth and practice licentiousness. (Art. XXXVII)

77

What this meant, of course, was that all really fundamental divergencies of both religion and thought were ruled out. This is no place to enter upon the vexed problem of toleration,[2] except to insist upon its relationship to the problem of constitutional reason of state, or "reason of commonwealth," since "freedom of religion" was one of the key rights and constitutive of constitutional thought and practice.[3]

But why include John Milton at all? Is he not a betrayer of the constitutional tradition? My answer would be that his thought shows clearly how from the very beginning constitutionalism contained a strand of radical constitutional reason of state, even though not so called and not recognized for its destructive potential.

In this connection, it is highly significant that Milton was the first to acknowledge a true "right of revolution," not merely in terms of resistance to a tyrant, but as a corollary of a free commonwealth. When I say that he was the first, I mean that no one before him proclaimed such a right in the name of progress and convenience:

Surely they that shall boast, as we do, to be a free nation, and not have in themselves the power to remove or abolish any gov-

[2] See for this the magistral work of W. K. Jordan, *The Development of Religious Toleration in England* (in four vols., 1932-1940). In this study Milton is dismissed with a couple of lines, vol. II, p. 30. The *Instrument,* on the other hand, is at length discussed; see especially vol. II, pp. 162 ff., and it is there shown that even this amount of "freedom of conscience" was endangered by parliamentary moves which were terminated by Cromwell who held this matter one of the "fundamentals" of the revolution.

[3] The well-known thesis of Georg Jellinek, *Die Erklärung der Menschenrechte* (1895, 1919 and later), while right in stressing the English origins of the doctrine of human rights, errs in insisting that the right to a free conscience (religious liberty) was the first of these to be won; the right of private property has a more ancient lineage, and certainly played its role in the English revolution.

ernor supreme, or subordinate, with the government itself upon urgent causes, may please their fancy with a ridiculous and painted freedom, fit to cozen babies; . . . (For without this) natural and essential power of a free nation, though bearing high their heads, they can in due esteem be thought no better than slaves and vassals, in the tenure and occupation of another inheriting lord; whose government, *though not illegal,* or intolerable, hangs over them as a lordly scourge, not as a free government; and therefore to be abrogated.[4]

Such revolutionary changes may be brought about by the people, because they "entertain a certain sense of happiness" and hence the people may "as oft as they judge it for the best, either choose or reject" a ruler, "though he be no tyrant" "merely by the liberty and right of free-born men to be governed as seems to them best." Here is the truly revolutionary note, the sense of a great mission "wherein we have the honour to precede other nations, who are now labouring to be our followers." Such a sense of a mission of transcending worth gives one the right to do what is necessary in order to accomplish one's God-given task. In a Christian and more especially in a Puritan garb it is the kind of inspiration which made Machiavelli feel the *rationale* of building that greatest work of art, a state.

Milton, naturally enough, avoids mention of the Machiavellian heritage. No pagan he, like his near-contemporary James Harrington. Indeed, in *Paradise Lost,* he was to coin the immortal phrases, pronounced by Satan:

> So spake the fiend, and with necessity
> The tyrant's plea, excused his devilish deeds.[5]

[4] *The Tenure of Kings and Magistrates* in *The Prose Works of John Milton,* with a Preface, preliminary remarks and notes by J. A. St. John, London (without date) in 5 vols., vol. II, pp. 33/4, italics mine. Other quotations from Milton are from the same edition.

[5] *Paradise Lost,* Book IV, lines 393-4. Merritt Y. Hughes, in his com-

But it may well be doubted whether Milton really wished to go back on the plea of necessity, employed at Pride's Purge, nor indeed on his necessitarian argument in *Eikonoklastes* and other commonwealth tracts.[6]

Milton had, in the beginning of the revolutionary upheaval, occasion to consider "reason of state" as such in another connection, namely in relation to *The Reason of Church Government* (1641). He there argued that "prelatical jurisdiction" is not only opposed to the Gospel, but also to "reason of state." It is all a matter of assuming governmental functions, instead of attending to their spiritual task and thereby "corrupting" the commonwealth, a "pestiferous contagion of the whole kingdom." The prelates are "the greatest underminers and betrayers of the monarch to whom they seem most favorable." Could it be that Milton was aware of Edward Dacres' translation of Machiavelli's *Prince,* published in 1640, who had concluded that if Cesare Borgia's "policy" had been "used for a good end, determined by God, it would have had a successful ending."[7] Such speculation may seem idle, except as it suggests the spread of reason of state thinking in Puritan circles before this time.

Specific reference may be made here to Philip Hunton, a significant figure in the developing constitutional thought. A vigorous advocate of mixed government, and more especially

---

mentary, rightly draws attention to the fact that this implies an oblique reference to the "reason of state" writings of the time.

[6] Perez Zagorin, in his interesting *A History of Political Thought in the English Revolution* (1954) pp. 82/6, draws attention to John Goodwin's defense of "necessity" in Pride's Purge, but declares it to be "fundamentally untenable." Is it really?

[7] See for this George L. Mosse, "Puritanism and Reason of State in Old and New England" *William and Mary Quarterly* (1952) p. 71. Mosse refers to Dacres' work at pp. 210-211.

of mixed monarchy, Hunton yet could not see how there could be any constitutional solution to a controversy between the several powers. His thought being still in terms of estates (resembling Sir Thomas Smith and others before him), Hunton thinks that such controversies are the "fatal disease of these governments,"[8] in that "it is a case beyond the possible provision of such a government." In other words, the idea of a constitutional framework, while spoken of, is somehow not seen in manageable, evolutionary terms, but as fixed and static. And yet, there is a glimmer. For "the accusing side must make it evident to every man's conscience," and "the appeal must be to the community, as if there were no government." It is evident that either in its application to England or in general terms, such a doctrine is not far enough advanced in a constitutional direction to develop a distinct reason of state.[9]

Such a doctrine as Milton's evidently was not an unravelling, but a cutting of the Gordian knot of constitutional reason of state. In any case, the question was bound to present itself: what if the belief, so dear to the Puritan revolutionaries,

[8] *Of Monarchical Government* (1643) pp. 28-9. See for Hunton the interesting discussion by Charles Howard McIlwain, *Constitutionalism and the Changing World* (1939) ch. IX.

[9] In his discussion of the prerogative Francis D. Wormuth, in his *The Royal Prerogative, 1603-1649* (1930) discusses Hunton, but not with reference to the prerogative. Note his interesting quote from John Saller (1649) anticipating Montesquieu's kind of separation of powers. But see Mosse, loc. cit., p. 74, who suggests that Hunton's use of the term "policy" implies a degnite awareness of "reason of state"; the references are, however, to the non-constitutional monarchy. The term "policy" has been used as a key for tracing Machiavelli's influence in Elizabethan England, but of course without any reference to the constitutional issue and purely as a literary matter; cf. the article by Napoleone Orsini, " 'Policy' or the Language of Elizabethan Machiavellianism," in *Journal of the Warburg and Courtauld Institute,* IX (1946) pp. 122-134, with references to such leading works as those of Mario Praz, Eduard Meyer and others.

should no longer be tenable or in fact held? This was the problem John Locke had to face, when he came to formulate *his* defense of the right of revolution. Milton had already claimed, as we have just shown, that a people have a right to fashion their government as they see fit, that they do not have to await the ruler turning tyrant, before seeking a basic change. His is the decisive turn. He did not merely repeat the older arguments which had always been cast in terms of removing a tyrant. But what Milton had claimed in passing and in the glow of revolutionary enthusiasm, John Locke made the mainstay of his argument.[10] The right of revolution is by him seen as altering the basic law and the form of government to suit the people, and is as such accepted. Yet, this right is at once surrounded by considerable safeguards. For it might easily mean anarchy. Among these safeguards, one in our context is of primary importance; Locke balances the "right of revolution" with the "prerogative." Now the prerogative was an ancient political and legal institution in Britain which had been much fought over in the beginning of the seventeenth century, more especially in the argument between King James I and Sir Edward Coke. Locke here, as so often, generalizes upon English constitutional thought. "Where the legislative and executive power are in distinct hands, as they are in all moderated monarchies and well-framed governments, there the good of the society requires that several things should be left to the discretion of him that has the executive power," he writes.[11]

[10] Cf. for John Locke, the magistral biography of A. R. Fox Bourne, *Life of John Locke* (2 vols., 1876); cf. also R. I. Aaron, *Locke* (1936 and 1955). The challenging argument of Willmore Kendall, *John Locke and the Doctrine of Majority Rule* (1941), does not invalidate the established view that Locke was, in spite of his, or rather one should say, because of his notion of the people as the constituent power, a prime expounder of constitutional thought.

[11] *Two Treatises on Government*, II, para. 159. This work is conven-

Locke presently defines the prerogative as "this power to act according to discretion for the public good, without the prescription of the law and sometimes even against it."[12] What does this metalegal prerogative comprise? Besides the discretion which implements the law, it also covers pardons which mitigate the law's severity, but more especially the power to act contrary to law when the public good requires it, that is to say, in emergencies. Locke goes on to point out that in the beginning of government, when it was paternal, most of it was "prerogative government," that is to say "government by discretion." But as prerogative was abused, and employed contrary to the public good, "the people were fain, by express laws, to get the prerogative determined." Such inroads of the law are not to be mistaken as encroachments. They are legitimate extensions implementing the constitution. But if the preregotive is a power to act contrary to the laws, when an emergency threatening the security and survival of the community demands it, what use is there in "determining" it by law? And what about the law of nature? Locke seems unwilling to say, though he would subject princes ordinarily to the natural law. Indeed, even God Almighty is, according to

---

tionally dated at 1689 or 1690, but it has recently been shown by Peter Laslett that it was written around 1680, immediately upon the publication of Filmer's *Patriarcha* against which it is directed. It is, in other words, more a call for than a defense of revolution. See for Laslett's views "The English Revolution and Locke's 'Two Treatises on Government'," *Cambridge Historical Journal,* XII (1956) pp. 40-55. This article constitutes part of a general introduction to a critical edition of the *Two Treatises,* soon to be published by the Cambridge University Press. Laslett has also given us a new edition of the *Patriarcha* with an illuminating introduction.

[12] Op. cit., ch. 160. For general background cf. Francis D. Wormuth, op. cit. It would lead too far afield to trace this doctrine in its legal ramifications.

Locke, bound by *paçta sunt servanda:* "Those rules are so great, so strong, in the case of promises, that omnipotency itself can be tied by them." In short, Locke, with his extraordinary capacity for allowing contradictions to stand, seems just to say: there is no solution, all one can do is to hope for the best. He leaves the reader rather unsatisfied. In good British fashion, he asks him to muddle through,—good princes have been allowed to interpret the prerogative broadly and somehow have managed.

By contrast with Locke, Rousseau would face the issue once more in terms of the Roman dictatorship. In view of his doctrine of the civil religion, he seems to belong among the pagans; yet there is no doubt that Rousseau was a Deist and would attribute the moral in man to God's revelation. In other words, his very important adaptation of the Roman doctrine of civil religion (as described by Polybius)[13] is rather poor theology; it shows, however, his appreciation of the transcendent ground of moral judgments and of the law derived from them. This is really the basis of his notion of the "general will," so much disputed about and still controversial.[14] For this term serves

[13] See Eberhard F. Bruck, *Über Römisches Recht im Rahmen der Kulturgeschichte* (1954), pp. 1 ff.

[14] For a more general discussion of the issue see my *Inevitable Peace* (1948), esp. ch. VI. The problem of the general will has been recently explored in considerable detail by Robert Derathé, *Jean Jacques Rousseau et la Science Politique de Son Temps* (1950), who arrives at the conclusion that Rousseau's conception of the general will is predominantly rational; cf. also the interesting article of Stanley Hoffman, "Du 'Contrat Social' ou le Mirage de la Volonté Générale," *Revue Internationale d'Histoire Politique et Constitutionelle*" (1955) pp. 228 ff. Derathé, in a recent article, "Les Refutations du Contrat Social au XVIIIe Siècle," *Annales de la Société J.-J. Rousseau*, XXXVI (1950-1952) pp. 7 ff., has shown how the general will provided a main point of attack for the Genevese prosecutor, M. Tronchin, because of its alleged subversive potential.

basically to re-introduce the rational into the political equation. Since the general will is said by Rousseau always to will the general good and to be always right, it must indeed be distinguished from the will of all, or of the majority which may err. Hence Rousseau expounds the concept of a "legislator," derived from classical antiquity, which he discusses in one of the most remarkable chapters of the *Contrat Social*.[15] This legislator, whose ultimate authority is charismatically derived from the Gods,—an idea which also occurs in Machiavelli in connection with the founding of states as Rousseau noted,— should have no other power, since he establishes the basic law; his office is neither magistracy nor sovereignty. This "legislator" must in no way be confused with the dictator, however; for the latter acts in emergencies after the body politic has come into being, while the former establishes the legal framework for it. The security and survival of the political order seem, in Rousseau's thought, to be treated in two radically divergent, indeed diametrically opposed ways, one the absolute rationality which prevails at the outset, and the other the equally absolute arbitrariness which watches over its continuance.[16] This arbitrariness, closely linked to Rousseau's

[15] Book II, ch. VII.

[16] In this connection, attention might be drawn to Rousseau's interest in the Polish system of handling emergencies, with the aid of the "confédération"—in fact a kind of vigilante group spontaneously formed in the face of emergency. Indeed, Rousseau went so far as to claim ("Gouvernement de Pologne," *Oeuvres de Jean-Jacques Rousseau,* ed. Mussay Pathay, 1826, vol. V, pp. 345ff.) that "confederation is in Poland what dictatorship was for the Romans." The argument is clearly in terms of security and survival. He acknowledges the violence involved, but thinks that "extreme ills make violent remedies necessary." He thinks that "confederation" has maintained the Polish constitution, while dictatorship destroyed the Roman one. From our viewpoint, the most important single line though is Rousseau's realization that "partout ou la liberté règne, elle est incessamment attaquée

conception of the general will, takes Rousseau out of the "constitutional" tradition. His celebrated passages on the real constitution that is graven on the hearts of the citizen refer not to a constitutional order in the strict sense, but to a general system of values and beliefs,—what some people nowadays would call an ideology. Since Rousseau completely subordinates the individual to the community as it expresses itself in the general will, the range of problems characteristic of constitutional reason of state did not present themselves to him. But they reappear in a new form in the philosophies of Kant and Hegel, both of course deeply influenced by Rousseau's political thought.

The reason for this paradox, which in its practical application led in the course of the French revolution from constitution-making to the terror, is ultimately rooted in Rousseau's failure to clarify the problem of the general will. For how are we to explain that a rational will is to emerge from majority decisions? Rousseau seeks to do it by an unexplained and romantic belief in the common man. Somehow, he is alleged to be animated by rational good sense. But in face of so much philosophical and practical evidence to the contrary, Rousseau's ardent assertions leave the reader unconvinced.

It is Kant (1724-1804) who comes to the rescue. By solving the problem of the general will in terms of the categorical imperative, as I have shown elsewhere,[17] he actually helps to

---

et très souvent en péril." And for this reason he is sure that without this institution of the "confédération," the Polish constitution would be destroyed, even if the *liberum veto* were to disappear. "Les confédérations sont le bouclier, l'asile, le sanctuaire de cette constitution," he insists, and therefore, rather than abolish them, it is necessary to regularize them by clarifying when and how they may operate. The American minutemen of the revolution may be said to have been an analogous institution.

[17] See *Inevitable Peace,* passim. H. J. Paton, in his closely reasoned

solve the problem of constitutional reason of state, though not entirely. Without attempting to go into the complex issues which the doctrine of the categorical imperative posits, we may say that the categorical imperative interprets man's moral judgments as being, in effect, general legislation.[18] Now, if most men, in acting morally, do in effect legislate, it is obvious that their several wills, when rational in this sense, will in practice coincide. One could test this in terms of the *pacta sunt servanda* rule: this rule is valid within the general context of the categorical imperative, because it is reasonable; but the very fact that whatever is done must be done in accordance with maxims that provide potentially universal legislation leaves open the door for subordinating the specific, though general rule of *pacta sunt servanda* to the still more general rule of self-preservation, i.e., of the security and survival of the constitutional order itself. But this does not mean a rejection of the rule; rather the sanctity of treaties becomes itself linked to the survival of the constitutional order. To put it another way: a constitutional order, a government of law, cannot survive, except by means of the scrupulous observation of the law; it is such observation of the law which ensures its success. In short, Kant does not say that something is right, because it is successful, as the secular survivalists tend to do, but asserts instead that since a certain line of conduct is right, it may be presumed that it has the potentiality or even the likelihood of succeeding. Few men involved in practical poli-

---

The Categorical Imperative (1948) does not deal with this aspect at all, but his analysis buttresses the point, by resolving some of the difficult problems of the doctrine.

[18] This is not the only form of the categorical imperative, of course, but perhaps the most important. Cf. Paton, op.cit., ch. XIV. Paton identifies five "formulas," cf. ch. XIII, et seq.

tics may care to adopt so optimistic a view, but it does provide a constitutional reason of state of simon-pure legality. In a sense, the solution resembles a Kantian argument in connection with the inherent rationality of historical events:

Even though we are too shortsighted to perceive the secret mechanism of nature's plan (regarding history), an otherwise planless *conglomeration* of human activities could be used as a guide when presented as a *system*. . . . By concentrating primarily on the civic constitution and its laws and on the relations among states, because both served to raise nations, their arts and sciences, one may discover a guide to explain the chaotic play of human affairs.

Therefore, the history of mankind could be viewed on the whole as the realization of a hidden plan of nature to bring about an internally and externally perfect constitution.[19] This perfect constitution is a constitution of mankind,—an universal order under law. Within its frame, culture will flourish. Even now the ambition of states forces them to maintain culture, the arts and sciences, because they are sources of strength.

Furthermore, civic freedom cannot now be interfered with without the state feeling the disadvantage of such interference in all trades . . . and as a result, a decline in power. . . . Eventually, even war will become a very dubious enterprise . . . other states will offer themselves as arbiters, and thus a future "great government" . . . will come into being. Even though this body politic at present is discernible only in its broadest outline, a sentiment in its favor is rising. . . .

Here, in 1784, in his *Idea for Universal History* Kant adumbrates what he later more fully developed in the famous essay on *Eternal Peace* (1795) as the *ultima ratio* of constitutionalism: a world federation under law. This conclusion was the

[19] See for a fuller development of this theme Ch. II, "The Idea of Progress in History and the Establishment of a Universal Order under Law" of my *Inevitable Peace*.

logical one to draw, if the problem of security and survival was to be solved within the context of constitutional thought. In essence, this conclusion asserts that the only escape from the conflict represented by reason of state thinking is the establishment of a system of universal law in which the problems of external and consequently of internal security are reduced to those of ordinary criminal law.[20] To the objection that such a rational end of history is undemonstrable, Kant answers that since its opposite is also undemonstrable, one might just as well choose the more pleasing alternative. Such a choice may at the same time aid its realization.

We see here that the rational implications of constitutional doctrine lead eventually to a point where the problem of constitutional reason of state loses its importance, because the "state" itself has been transcended in an international order of a federal type.[21] Once more, the inherent dialectic of constitutional reason of state has been resolved by an ingenuous process of elimination, but the Kantian solution has the advantage of providing a developmental model and a pragmatic, if not a practical projection into the future, by which concrete political action programs may be inspired and policy shaped.

In conclusion, we can say that the moralists' approach to constitutional reason of state also undergoes a significant evolution. Milton, Locke, Kant,—they are all cognizant of the significant role of revolution and hence of dynamic change

[20] The quotes are taken from my *The Philosophy of Kant,* pp. 127-131. The original may be consulted in Cassierer's edition of the *Werke,* vol. IV, pp. 161-166.

[21] For my view of the federal aspect of this problem see *Constitutional Government and Democracy,* loc. cit., ch. XI, and the chapter in Arthur MacMahon (ed), *Federalism, Mature and Emergent* (1955), entitled "Federal Constitutional Theory and Emergent Proposals," where the communal basis of federalism is shown to be decisive.

in the political order. Reason of state cannot be merely the maintenance of the status quo; it must be expressive of a mode or modes of progressive change. But whereas this progressive change is, by Milton, placed in charge of a "Christian nation" which will show the world how to build a Christian commonwealth, Locke sees it as the ultimate legitimation of the political order by any people, composed of reasonable men. Both would leave to the effective and representative leader the task of choosing the necessary means. These means will be rational, will be "reason of state," because of the inherent moral rationality of the men employing it. For Kant, more sceptical of men and their works, more convinced of the coercive aspect of all government, including constitutional government, the notion of a progressive realization of constitutionalism depends upon constitutionalism's effective expansion. It must come to embrace the world so as to unite a mankind represented by the rationality of a will shaped by the categorical imperative in general, and more particularly by that imperative which declares: there shall not be war. Constitutional order organizes mankind as a federal community embracing all men.

Hegel

Reason of State as Reason of History

IN THE WORK OF HEGEL, the two approaches, the secular and the Christian slant, converge and appear to be reconciled. But does Hegel really belong in a discussion of constitutional reason of state? We find Meinecke devoting one of his most challenging chapters to Hegel, placing him squarely in the tradition of state absolutism.[1] Similarly, and more radically, it was argued by others that Hegel was a representative of the idea of the power state,—the state interpreted in terms of pure power (*Machtstaatsgedanke*),—with particular emphasis on Hegel's early study of the German constitution.[2] Such inter-

[1] See Friedrich Meinecke, op. cit., Book III, ch. I. Meinecke gives undue weight to Hegel's early views as expressed in his essay on the German constitution, and builds the argument essentially on the work of Herrmann Heller, *Hegel und der Nationale Machtstaatsgedanke in Deutschland* (1921), with which he notes some disagreement, and on Franz Rosenzweig, *Hegel und der Staat* (2 vols. 1920). Cf. for a recent contrasting treatment Eric Weil, *Hegel et l'Etat* (1950), as well as the remarkable studies by Jean Kojève, *Introduction à la Lecture de Hegel Leçons sur la Phénoménologie de l'Esprit* (1947). For other literature on Hegel see my Introduction to *The Philosophy of Hegel* (1953) where a brief extract and comment on the Constitution essay is found, p. 527ff.

[2] Cf. Heller, op. cit., especially pp. 32-57. Heller identifies *Macht* and *Machtstaat,* even though none of the quotes from Hegel supports such an identification, and naturally not, since for Hegel the state in its true essence is a *Rechtsstaat.*

pretations helpfully brought out the importance of power in Hegel's thinking, but they overstressed it, since the power Hegel demanded for a state was clearly that required for the realization of law and general spiritual values, and not the natural force contrary to these manifestations of the spirit. Nor are we justified in using Hegel's views as expressed in a moment of deepest national crisis for the purpose of interpreting his thought as a whole. To equate his thought with that of Treitschke, merely because Hegel insisted that a formal order such as the Holy Roman Empire was, since it lacked power, no state: this is not permissible. Treitschke, himself a historian, always felt very critical of Hegel. For Hegel's thought is deeply inspired by the notion of government according to law, and the corresponding idea that such a government provides the framework for the realization of freedom.[3]

Hegel shows in a number of key works, but more especially in his *Philosophy of History*,[4] quite clearly that he considered the constitutional state, as represented by the British monarchy of the eighteenth century and what he hoped the Prussian and

[3] Rosenzweig, op.cit., shows how this idea gradually evolved in Hegel's thought on the state, and that it constitutes the heart of his philosophy.

[4] *Die Vernunft in der Geschichte—Einleitung in die Philosophie der Weltgeschichte* constitutes the first and most generally studied part of Georg Friedrich Wilhelm Hegel's *Vorlesungen ueber die Philosophie der Geschichte,* the original edition of which in *Hegels Werke,* based on lecture notes, was translated by J. Sibree under the title *Philosophy of History* in 1901 and has recently been republished by Dover Publications. However, since that time, Georg Lasson edited a critical edition (2.ed., 1920) in which he was able to identify a brief introduction written by Hegel himself, Lasson having discovered this MS. Most of this genuine Hegel version is included in my edition mentioned in the previous footnote. Since Lasson's time, Johannes Hoffmeister gave us a number of works in still more refined critical editions; unfortunately this painstaking scholar died before the philosophy of history could be completed, though we have his edition of the introduction. As a memento, I should like to mention here his masterly and illuminating

other monarchies would become in his day, to be superior to any *Machtstaat,* or absolutist government. In a celebrated passage, implemented by a long footnote in his *Philosophy of Law and Right* he castigated mercilessly a writer who had recently expounded the idea of such a state, based on brute power (*Macht*) rather than law.[5] This writer's notion that it is God's unalterable order that "the more powerful rule, must rule and always will rule" elicits from Hegel the revealing observation that clearly the author's examples show that what he means is natural power or force, not the power of the just and the ethical. From which it becomes very evident that for Hegel it is only the just and ethical power which is embodied in a true state. It is, therefore, entirely inadmissible to say that "the actual state is the rational state."[6] On the contrary, Hegel had a very vivid sense of the conflict between his ideal concept, and the ugly distortions of it that are found all around us. "The state exists in the world, and hence in the sphere of the arbitrary, of accident, and error. Evil behavior can disfigure it in many ways. But the ugliest man, the criminal, the invalid, the cripple, are still living men."[7] Hegel explicitly states that he is not concerned with the historical state, nor

---

critical edition of *Hegel's Briefwechsel,* in four volumes. These critical editions are specially noted. General references to Hegel's works are to the original edition as republished by Glockner; these references are preceded by a G.

[5] Cf. *Grundlinien der Philosophie des Rechts* (rev.ed. by Johannes Hoffmeister, 1955) pp. 210-15; the writer in question is von Haller, and his work *Restauration der Staatswissenschaft.*

[6] This is the position taken by Meinecke, op. cit., pp. 434. Meinecke then quotes Hegel's "Was vernuenftig ist, das ist wirklich; und was wirklich ist, das ist vernuenftig," taking no account of Hegel's own commentary to the contrary. Cf. for a sound analysis W. T. Stace, *The Philosophy of Hegel* (1923), esp. para. 607 and 608.

[7] This statement is from the "additions" (or *Zusaetze*) given by Eduard Gans in 1833, and eliminated from Hoffmeister's critical edition (as indeed previously by Lasson).

with its historical origin. "The philosophical analysis (*Betrachtung*) has to do only with the inner side (*Inwendigen*) of all this, with the concept that is thought." He criticizes Rousseau, because he did not conceive of the general will as that which is in-and-of-itself rational in the will, though insisting that Rousseau deserves praise for having formulated the will as the principle of the state. For Hegel, however, the content of the will is "thought," or rather will is "thinking itself." This "error" of Rousseau led to the French revolution, a "terrible spectacle," involving the attempt to construct a constitution "from the very beginning" by giving it as a foundation "the supposedly rational" which was in fact "abstractions devoid of ideas." For Hegel "the objective will is what is in its very concept rational, whether it is recognized by men and wanted by their desire or not." Likewise, the true state is the rational ethical kernel or core, whereas the various historical aspects of existing states, their strength or weakness, their wealth or poverty, etc., are only the "rind" which thought must pierce with its concepts in order to discover the true reality which is "infinite."[8] He then turns to the vigorous criticism of von Haller who had expounded the *Machtstaat* notions which Meinecke (and many others following him) wish to impute to Hegel.

And yet, there is a reason for this ever-recurrent misunderstanding, and it is to be found in Hegel's philosophy of history and in the role assigned to the state in this philosophy which is responsible for them. For Meinecke certainly is right when he claims that Hegel's concept of reason was a new one which could not "founder" on the contradictions and on the seem-

---

[8] Cf. *Grundlinien* (ed. Hoffmeister) pp. 209/10. Not all of these and previous quotes are found in my edition as cited. Cf. the, in many ways, excellent translation by Knox with whom I differ on some key concepts, unfortunately.

ingly unresolved conflicts of life and history, because "by means of its dialectic it comprehended these conflicts as necessary means of progress and thus sanctioned the entire causal nexus of history with all its dark and horrible abysses."[9] History provides the stage upon which the great drama of mankind's spiritual liberation is played. This spiritual liberation is closely linked with the development of the state. For the state, as that being which is rational in-and-of-itself, provides for men the chance to be free; only through participating in a state can they be free, and hence it is their "highest duty" to be members of a state. But this is true only because the existing states embody, as it were, the idea of the state, as expressed in these statements. Above all this is true of the constitutional states of his time in which Hegel saw a nearer approximation to the idea which the world spirit had been at work to realize through history.

The road to this conception leads from Montesquieu to Hegel. It has not been noted sufficiently how much Hegel, who always acknowledged his admiration for Montesquieu,[10] is

[9] Meinecke says "for the first time," but actually the same idea is found, as we showed in a previous chapter, in Kant's essay *Idee zu einer Allgemeinen Geschichte* . . . (1784); indeed, it is rooted in earlier religious notions tracing to St. Augustine and the Old Testament; cf. my *Inevitable Peace*, ch. III.

[10] There are numerous references to Montesquieu, e.g. Hegel, *Sämtliche Werke*, hrsg. von H. Glockner (1927-1939), 26 vols., I, 531; VI, 406; VII, 43 & 48; VII, 339; VII, 373-375; X, 84; XI, 328-9; XI, 32; XIX, 514, 519, 525 and XX, 475. Further references to this edition are prefixed by G. For our purposes, the most important references are in the *Philosophy of History,* where Montesquieu is described as a particular type of historian, the reflective, and in the *Philosophy of Right and Law,* where Hegel especially notes that Montesquieu's great contribution lay in the fact that he described law and legislation in relation to the totality of culture,—the character of a nation, as he put it. See for this Hildegard Trescher, "Montesquieu's Einfluss auf die Philosophischen Grundlagen der Staatslehre Hegels," *Schmollers Jahrbuch* . . . 1917.

following Montesquieu's general approach when he conceives law and government,—and the two are always linked in Montesquieu's as in Hegel's thought,—as the expression of a "general spirit." Only in Montesquieu, these spirits are, as we saw, treated as an un-ordered *Nebeneinander* on which he superimposes his rational dichotomy of despotic and constitutional systems, whereas in Hegel they are made part of an ordered historical procession which is ultimately shaped and directed by the world spirit through which God is manifest in history. In short, the link between Montesquieu's *Esprit des Lois* and Hegel's *Philosophy of History* is to be found in the emphasis on the "spirit." Spirit, while linked to reason, is yet something more elevated and more personalized. More especially the world spirit which manifests itself in a succession of folk spirits,—incidentally Hegel's world-historical peoples are not so much nations as civilizations,—has one dominant end, and that is the realization of freedom. This freedom, of course, possesses a very special sense which Hegel gives to the concept, that is to say, it is closely related to law. For "law is altogether freedom, as an idea." "The legal order is the realm of actualized freedom"; it is "the world of the spirit as created by the will."[11] It is for this reason that "law is something *sacred altogether,* simply because it is the being of the absolute concept, of self-conscious freedom." Only such free will is rational, and only such rational free will is general, and hence truly related to the idea of the state. Freedom, in turn, is most fully embodied in the constitutional government which the "Germanic" peoples, the British, the Dutch, the Scandinavian, the German, yes, even the French and Spanish peoples have

[11] *Rechtsphilosophie,* ed. Hoffmeister, p. 28 and ff. The next quote is from p. 46 (para. 4, 29 and 30 particularly). Italics in Hegel quotations are Hegel's own.

worked out. What then of the constitutional reason of state?

"If we did not know that Hegel had, since his youth, worked on the problems of politics, along with those of the world of religion, with the searching intensity typical of him, his *Rechtsphilosophie,*—which is nothing but his doctrine of the objective spirit,—would clearly show us that many of his basic thoughts matured in looking at this part of existence."[12] And yet, with all this intense interest in government, politics and the state, the concept of "reason of state" does not play any significant role in Hegel's thinking. And his appreciation of Machiavelli, though real, was quite limited, as indeed might be suspected. For Hegel explicitly refers only to Machiavelli's *Prince,* and in regard to this work he stresses national unification as a task which needs no justification and with regard to which the argument about whether the end justifies the means is meaningless. His argument is built upon the notion that the situation of sixteenth century Italy and hence the proposals of Machiavelli closely parallel the problem of Germany in 1800. Herder had taken a similar line. There can be no doubt that Hegel, for the solution of this problem, was willing to accept a conqueror who would gather the "common crowd of the German people," including their estates, into "one mass." They must be forced to consider themselves as Germans.[13] But even at this early stage in the development of his thought, he insists that such a Theseus must have the generosity to grant the people a participation in what concerns all. This is in line

[12] Theodor Litt in his recent *Hegel—Versuch einer Kritischen Erneuerung* (1953) p. 99.
[13] Der gemeine Haufe des deutschen Volkes nebst ihren Landständen . . . müsste durch die Gewalt eines Eroberers in Eine (sic) Masse versammelt, sie müssten gezwungen werden, sich zu Deutschland gehörig zu betrachten." *Hegels Schriften zur Politik und Rechtsphilosophie* (ed. Georg Lasson, p. 135).

with Hegel's characteristic observation that Machiavelli made truly idealistic demands upon a good prince. Only the task of national unification explains the evil counsels which he offers, whereas Machiavelli's genuine concern, the viewing of the state as a work of art, as a deliberate creation of an heroic legislator (see above, ch. II), is far removed from Hegel's conception of it as "the actual reality of the ethical idea." It is not difficult to imagine the mocking smile which would have passed over the Florentine thinker's face, if he had been told of Hegel's metaphysical speculations.[14] And yet, Hegel had an appreciation of Machiavelli's view, at least as far as the local Italian situation was concerned. Italy, he says, was divided into many principalities, and hence the papacy emerged dominant. For such subjection to the papacy there existed a "right in the ethical sense." This right is revealed by Machiavelli's *Prince.* "Often one has with disgust condemned this book, as filled with the maxims of the most cruel tyranny. But in the high sense of the necessity of the formation of a state Machiavelli formulated the principles according to which under such circumstances states had to be formed. The separate rulers and their domains had to be suppressed. We cannot accept, considering our concept of freedom, the means which he suggests

---

[14] Hegel to my knowledge mentions Machiavelli four times in his writings. The first and most extended discussion occurs in his essay on the constitution of Germany, as cited in the previous footnote. Here he quotes the *Prince* at some length, after having recalled the division of Italy and her desperate plight in face of foreign aggression. Note also the discussion below. The second mention occurs in his *History of Philosophy,* where he speaks of Machiavelli rather lightly together with such others as Montaigne as interesting writers, commentators on life and politics, but without philosophical interest (G, XIX, 252); yet another one in his study of the doings of the estates of Wuerttemberg (ibid., 354), and the final one in the philosophy of history as cited in the text. The passages are found in G, XI, 509/10, and occur within the context of the discussion of the Middle Ages.

as the only available and completely justified ones, because they include the most ruthless violence, all kinds of deception, murder and so forth. But we must admit, that the rulers which had to be suppressed could only thus be attacked, because an inflexible lack of conscience and a complete corruption were thoroughly characteristic of them." This is, of course, reason of state reasoning. But it is very limited in scope and application, and it refers in no way to the problems peculiar to a constitutional order. These particular difficulties which Machiavelli only touched upon in his *Discourses,* Hegel did especially discuss only once. It is, however, demonstrable that his preference for a constitutional *monarchy* was indicative of his basic notions in this respect.

The one explicit discussion of the problems of internal security as such occurs significantly within the context of the discussion of Machiavelli and the unification of Italy touched upon above. The detestable means which Machiavelli advocated for dealing with the enemies of the unification should, Hegel suggests, be seen as punishments for treason. "What would be detestable when done by one private man against another, or one state against another, is just punishment (in this case). To cause anarchy is the greatest, indeed the only crime against a state . . . they who attack the state directly are the greatest criminals, and the state has no higher duty than to preserve itself and to destroy the power of such criminals."[15] It would seem that at least at this early stage in his political thought Hegel was prepared to grant the state limitless and arbitrary power, when its own defense and self-preservation is at stake. But it is interesting that this issue is not resumed in his mature *Philosophy of Right and Law,* where the rational state is seen as the constitutional state in modern parlance.

[15] *Die Verfassung Deutschlands* (1802) loc. cit., p. 113/4.

Hegel himself uses the term constitution in a broad sense, like the ancients, to designate any political organization in which a large sphere is left to "civil society" and its members and in which a separation of powers has been developed so as to enable the citizens to participate effectively in the making of laws.[16] But in order to avoid the dissolution of the state's power by such a separation which had recurrently been criticized, Hegel suggested that each of the powers must be a "totality," that is to say, in each of them all the others must likewise be at work. Recognizing the general dissatisfaction that constitutionalism in its rationalist form as popularized by the French revolution had occasioned, Hegel insists that a philosophical understanding of constitutionalism can only be gathered from the *concept* (and not from either utility or sentiment and emotion). The separation of powers is indeed the guarantee of public (political) liberty, for this principle is derived from the rational difference of the several governmental activities. But it must not be misunderstood either in the sense that these powers are absolutely autonomous or independent (*selbstständig*), or that they are to limit each other. For such negative conception is based upon the notion of a hostility of these powers against each other, resulting in a balance and not in a unity.[17] In keeping with such an outlook, Hegel abandoned the traditional division and separation once again for a scheme more nearly like that of Locke: he distinguished three powers

[16] Cf., *Philosophie des Rechts.*, para. 272 ff. (ed. Hoffmeister, pp. 233 ff.)

[17] That Hegel's view of the separation of powers is based upon the Kantian notion, which had interpreted the separation of the legislative, the executive and the judicial power as parallel to and conforming to a syllogism, is obvious. But Kant had given it in Hegel's view this "negative" turn which he wished to avoid by not only interpreting holistically the state as a whole, but the separated powers as well.

of which the first is the legislative which determines and establishes the general (rules), the second the governmental power which subsumes the particular spheres and individual cases under the general[18] and the third the princely or monarchical power which makes the final decision of the will. In this last power the powers as distinguished are brought together and unified; it is therefore both the pinnacle and the base of the entire constitutional structure. It is evident that this monarchical power is the distinctive element of Hegel's constitutionalism.[19] For him, the development of the state into a constitutional monarchy is the achievement of the modern world. Hence the history of this achievement, the history of this "true *Gestaltung* (formation, organization and structuring) of ethical life" is the theme of general world history. Before we turn to this aspect of the matter, two points call for clarification. One is Hegel's view that the classification of governments into monarchy, aristocracy and democracy was natural for the classical world which had not yet achieved the degree of concrete rationality which a constitutional system presupposes. In a constitutional monarchy, these several forms have become aspects (*Moments*) of the political order; but their numerical aspect is unimportant. The simple forms have only historical significance; there is no sense in disputing about their relative worth. Hegel then discusses sympathetically Montesquieu's notion about the quality which is desirable for

[18] The text reads "und," but the sense calls for "unter."
[19] This recognition of a separate monarchical power, reminiscent of Locke's federative power which was strictly monarchical, too, constitutes a key feature of Benjamin Constant's constitutional theory which Hegel strongly approved and was presumably influenced by. Cf. the testimony of Hegel's early biographer, Karl Rosenkranz, *Georg Friedrich Wilhelm Hegels Leben* (1844). The key work of Constant is *Cours de Droit Constitutionel* (1814).

each form: virtue for democracy, moderation for aristocracy and honor for monarchy, but suggests that virtue *and* moderation are needed for a constitutional monarchy. This highly differentiated constitution is therefore not exactly a mixture, but a new synthesis; it develops organically and cannot be made. In terms familiar from Burke, Hegel states that it is "absolutely essential that a constitution though emerging in time be *not* considered as *something made.*" Indeed, a constitution is "divine, that which exists absolutely of-and-by-itself."[20]

The other point concerns the monarchical power itself. It is essential to a constitutional order, because it provides the necessary unity. In the monarch, the unity of the state, the people's personality is personified. Without him, it remains a "formless mass" which is no state. Hence Hegel rejects the idea of popular sovereignty as "confused" and based upon a *"wild* notion of a *people."* Popular sovereignty makes sense only in relation to the outside world. All this rests upon Hegel's concept of state sovereignty which finds its expression in the person of the monarch. "The personality of the state is actual only as a person, the monarch."[21] His will, which is a rational will, provides the unity of the state, and because this will is not "moved by arbitrary freedom (*Willkür*) it constitutes the *majesty* of the monarch." To support this idealized view of the monarch and his will, Hegel recalls the analogous reasoning in the ontological proof of the existence of God, and admits

[20] See also Hegel, *Philosophie der Geschichte* (ed. Lasson) p. 121, also 103.

[21] It may not be amiss to recall that this is essentially the argument of Hobbes, e.g. in ch. XVI of *Leviathan,* where he deals with representation. The argument also shows how sharply Hegel's conception of the state as the precondition of a "people" diverges from Hitler's notions which correspond precisely to what Hegel called "wild notions of a people." Cf. Hegel as cited above fn (20), pp. 243-247.

that in both cases an act of speculative reason is involved: the immediate transformation (*unmittelbare Umschlagen*) of the "pure self-determination of the will, that is to say the simple concept itself, into a something here and now (*ein Dieses*) and a natural existence." These presumably deep, but somewhat obscure formulations provide the basis for Hegel's solution of the problem of constitutional reason of state, and a highly idealistic and unsatisfactory solution it is. Presumably whenever the security and survival of the state is at stake, whether threatened by foreign or by internal foes, the monarchical power will step into the breach and do what is necessary. It is clear that Hegel's solution is very similar to Locke's doctrine of the prerogative (see above, ch. V). It resolves the problem by denying it.

But in order to grasp more fully the philosophical and political significance of Hegel's "solution," we must return to his philosophy of history. We had seen that the modern constitutional state, its *Gestaltung* or organization of ethical life, was the crowning achievement of world history. And contemporary Prussia, with its powerful ruler and its enlightened if arrogant bureaucracy, seemed to the philosopher a more effective embodiment of this achievement, as did other constitutional monarchies of the continent, France, Austria, Bavaria, than did Britain which was afflicted by corruption and lacked an effective government service. To give the devil his due, one might recall that the British were at the time of Hegel's death getting ready to remedy this grave defect. All this is, however, detail in comparison to the inherent "deification" of the state[22] which results from Hegel's metaphysic of history. This metaphysic makes

[22] This term, perhaps a bit overly dramatic, is in fact sanctioned by Rosenzweig, the most profound analyst of Hegel's concept of the state. Op. cit., *passim*.

history a manifestation of the world spirit, itself the expression of God's will and hence in truth a theodicee.[23] To state briefly the familiar line of argument, the world spirit works through folk spirits *(Volksgeister)* which in turn shape the culture, in all its branches, and more especially the state. The state, as legally organized power, is thus the most important instrument in the hand of God. Whatever is necessary for the success of the realization of the historical mission of such a spirit, which is the spirit of a world-historical people *(Volk*—not simply to be identified with the modern "nation" as already noted), that also is sanctioned as moral in the deepest sense. Not merely the big fish devour the little ones by natural law and right, as in Spinoza, but the coming culture destroys the antecedent one, the coming form of political order supersedes the antecedent one by "natural law and right." The kinship, as well as the contrast with Spinoza is striking. Might once again makes right, but it is not the static might of nature, but the dynamic might of history.[24] Thus security and survival become incidents of the historical process: world History renders the final judgment, it is the universal court[25] to which all these questions are ultimately submitted. Such questions, therefore, turn upon where one stands in the historical process, and the victor ap-

[23] See the last paragraphs of *Die Philosophie der Geschichte* where Hegel says that history is "God's work."

[24] Note the interesting remarks of Hegel concerning the possible future role of Americans and Russians in the *Philosophy of History* and elsewhere, as cited in my *The Philosophy of Hegel,* Introduction, pp. LIII-LIV.

[25] I should like to note here in passing that the famous formula associated with Hegel's name that world history is the world court actually comes from Friedrich Schiller's poem *Die Resignation* where it is part of Schiller's lines: "Geniesse, wer nicht glauben kann. Die Lehre ist ewig, wie die Welt. Wer glauben kann, entbehre!" Hoffen und glauben, hope and faith, are the two alternatives and "was man von der Minute ausgeschlagen, gibt keine Ewigkeit zurueck."

pears always right. For the time being, all the guidance one has is one's faith in the future; whether an action is ultimately "right" or "wrong" can only be determined in retrospect.

There is, however, some doubt in Hegel's mind about so unmitigated a success philosophy. In the Introduction to *The Philosophy of History* he recognizes the moral worth of the gallant lost cause. The reason is that what the final end of the spirit requires cannot be made the basis of individual ethics. Hence "those who have resisted what was made necessary by the progression of the idea of the spirit, who have done so out of ethical considerations and hence noble conviction, are morally superior to those whose crimes were converted by a higher order into means for carrying out the will of this high order." And yet, we ought to abstain from applying to the instruments of the world spirit, of God's will in history, these ethical standards of individual conduct. "Moral circles ought not to object to world historical deeds and those who accomplish them." The reason is that "the deeds of great men who are world-historical individuals thus appear justified not only in their inner and to them unknown meaning, but also from the world standpoint." In this context of the higher plane of history, the stage of the world spirit, Hegel suggests that the world spirit "could dispense entirely with the sphere to which morality and the oft-discussed conflict between morals and politics belongs."[26] This could be done "by abstaining from such (moral) judgments" and indeed "by omitting altogether reference to individuals."

Constitutional reason of state has absolute claims against the individual, and these claims may, therefore, in fact be relegated to the limbo of a "formalism" which is concerned with

[26] These passages are found in my selections, p. 31. Cf. Lasson's critical edition, p. 153 (they form part of Hegel's own MS).

"the litany of private virtues, such as modesty, humane love and gentleness." "For what world history is reporting are the deeds of the spirit of the peoples. . . ." By such a train of reasoning, constitutional reason of state becomes a part of that universal reason which is at work in the world spirit. And yet, Hegel would assign to the individual, too, an absolute value. In the world-historical context, the individual may be merely a means to an end, but "there is nonetheless in every individual a side which we hesitate to view this way." This side is their morality, their ethics, their religion. These are something "intrinsically eternal and divine." Man, through what is thus divine in him, is an end in himself; and this divine element in him is what always has been called reason, and, when active, freedom. In so far as individuals possess them, they are removed from the causal nexus; as they lose them, as religion and morals become corrupt and decline, the individuals become guilty and are doomed. That these are modern formulations of the ancient *virtue* ideal, much as Hegel's view of history is secularized Christian providence (even containing analogous paradoxes), that they resemble what we find in earlier political thought, merely highlights their basic importance for constitutional reason of state. Hegel is metaphysically convinced that the "reason" at work in individuals is the same "reason" at work in history. He finds rather moving, poetical expressions for this sentiment, as far as the individual is concerned. "The religion, the ethics of the restricted life, the life of a shepherd or peasant has infinite value in its concentrated intensity." Indeed, he does not hesitate to claim for it the same value as for the religion, the spiritual life of the most advanced. "This inward center, this simple sphere of the right of subjective freedom . . . remains untouched by the loud noise of world history."[27]

[27] See my Selections, pp. 18/20; cf. Lasson's edition, pp. 84-89.

To conclude, Hegel's doctrine of the "reason of state" or more especially "reason of the rational state," that is to say, the constitutional state, is given its radical turn by the spiritualizing of power, of might, by the interpretation of the state as an ethical individual being, by the broader philosophical interpretation, in other words, of the state as not only the necessary condition, but as the very embodiment of *nomos,* of right conduct. Here is the decisive flaw in Hegel's thought: in the confusing of right and might. Hegel himself might explain that he meant to deny the true existence of that which is not reasonable, when he wrote that whatever is actual, is reasonable.[28] The fact remains that we return with him to a position in the matter of constitutional reason of state which resembles Machiavelli's. The deified, the sanctified state as the end of all political activity is given so transcendent a value that the means for its preservation do not need any justification. They are implied in this end, and are thus "suspended, superseded and preserved."[29] But as we have tried to show, Hegel is not at ease with this dominant strand in his thought. There is an individualist *motif* which contradicts it and provides a genuine dialectic. In the perspective of this his ultimate regard for the ethical man, rather than the ethical state, Hegel belongs into the camp of those Christians for whom reason of state was so peculiarly tough a problem. Thus not only *Diamat,* the dialectical materialism of Soviet propaganda, but also contrasting ideologies of movements and states recognizing the dignity of man often bear the stamp of the Hegelian dialectic of history and its constitutional reason of state.

[28] As he did in the foreword to the second edition of the *Enzyklopaedie der Wissenschaften;* cf. for this point my introduction, op. cit., pp. L-LI.

[29] On the complexities of the Hegelian term "aufheben," see my introduction, as cited, and the literature there referred to, but more especially Kojève, *passim.*

VII   Conclusion

FROM MACHIAVELLI TO HEGEL, security and survival of the state and more especially of the good state, of the constitutional, civilized political order had challenged the ingenuity of the best minds. No clear-cut, definite answer had crystallized by the beginning of the nineteenth century. When constitution-*making* commenced in earnest, those who were framing the new charters, tended to fall back upon the Lockean escape into some kind of monarchical prerogative. War powers with its martial law, the state of siege and so-called emergency powers followed later, often working reasonably well, but at times, as in the case of the ill-constructed Art. 48 of the Weimar constitution, wreaking havoc and destroying the very fabric which such powers were meant to preserve.[1] But it was only the latter experience,—Mussolini's March on Rome was another,—which really high-lighted the problem of security and survival of a constitutional order in its gravest form, namely, when occurring in the setting of a totalitarian challenge. Not that the problem of internal subversion was novel, even though it had been attenuated in the halcyon days of

[1] Cf. for the most authoritative treatment, Frederick M. Watkins, *The Failure of Constitutional Emergency Powers under the German Republic* (1939); cf. also C. L. Rossiter's *Constitutional Dictatorship* (1948).

nineteenth century liberalism. We have seen that it played a role in the thought of the past at practically every stage. But internal subversion which seeks to establish another constitutional frame, or which seeks to re-establish an older traditional authoritarian order is not the same deadly threat that totalitarian movements have proved to be. As a consequence, we find contemporary constitutional systems evolving a variety of new approaches. The threat of total war and total destruction through A-bombs, H-bombs, bacteriological warfare raises even more desperate issues, but little has been done or even proposed to prepare existing constitutional states for such an ordeal.[2] We shall, therefore, in this conclusion concentrate on the internal aspect.

If we review the thought of the past, we find that the fundamental issue has been answered in a number of ways. Let us restate this fundamental issue once more as follows: How can one, how must one deal with declared enemies, not only of the established, but of any constitutional order, who yet as citizens are entitled to the protection of the constitution, and more especially are beneficiaries of its guarantee of basic human rights or civil liberties? There are those who would, in line with a long tradition, going back to Milton and Calvin, outlaw such persons, deprive them of their status as citizens and exile or suppress them (put them into camps, perhaps, as the McCarren Act proposes to do with Communists and "fellow-travelers" in wartime). There are others who would organize a special tribunal or would entrust an existing one to deal with the task of identifying such elements and of de-

[2] A notable exception is Clinton Rossiter's proposal for a temporary presidential dictatorship of sweeping competence; Cf. Rossitter, *Review of Politics,* Vol. IX, 1949, p. 395. However, this proposal is not contained in his recent study of the presidency.

priving them of some of their liberties. Emergency powers, that is some species of constitutional dictatorship, have many advocates, as they had in the writings we have examined. There are, however, others who would trust, as Locke had done, to a constitutional order's inherent strength, as long as there is somewhere a "prerogative" of sorts. Still others essentially side with Hegel, thinking that it is all more or less a matter of spiritual force (or some material or biological equivalent thereof), and that nothing much can be done, except to understand these historical forces at work. Finally, there are those who with Kant would consider the problem as essentially unresolvable except within the context of an universal order under law, of a constitutionally organized peace that will be "everlasting."

If we glance once more at the historical evolution of the ideas involved, we perceive an interesting pattern. For one, many of the thinkers on constitutional reason of state freely acknowledge their indebtedness to Machiavelli, rather than denouncing him, as was the fashion especially in the seventeenth century. They seem to realize that here was a writer who, whatever his faults and his astigmatism, faced with laudable rigor the problem of security and survival. But while he faced it, he did not really advance it beyond praising the institution of the Roman dictatorship. This was due to his failure to grasp the legal aspect of constitutional government, attached as he was to its libertarian potential.

Three thinkers undertook to develop the Machiavellian heritage in this field, Harrington, Spinoza and Montesquieu. Harrington, with his passion for institutional detail, generalized the Venetian institution of a security council, the dictatorian as he called it, with discretionary powers of ill-defined scope. Spinoza would allow the government all the range of operation which its power would permit it, but insisted upon the rationale of a sphere of individual liberty involved. Montesquieu, troubled by the Roman experience, and facing the despotic potential of contemporary absolutism, believed that a proper amending process could keep the basic law in step with the requirements of the situation, while at the same time arguing for the importance of executive leadership, if suitably restrained by "intermediary powers." This explicitly Machiavellian strand of thought on constitutional reason of state culminated in Hegel, but so did a contrasting strand which is explicitly or implicitly based on the Christian tradition.

Calvin, the Calvinists and Althusius more particularly, conceiving of themselves as "God's people," sanctified the inherent *rationale* of politics by seeing it frankly as the politician's calling. When extended to include the citizen at large, as is done by Althusius and later Calvinists, this calling and its rationale become embedded in a concept of emergency powers, to be deployed against tyrants and other subversives, at the discretion of the people's representatives. From here, the road leads to Milton's right of revolution; none of these "warriors of the Lord" have any doubt that the saints will act in accordance with the laws for whose realization they are fighting. The problem of constitutional reason of state is, in a sense, resolved in terms of a transcendent faith in the member of a Christian constitutional community, the "commonwealth."

Locke, less sure of the sanctity of the constituency, but more optimistic about man in general, takes refuge in generalizing the traditional English doctrine of the "prerogative." In short, he believes that in every constitutional order fit to survive there must somewhere be somone who can do whatever the emergency situation requires,—an outlook still dominant in the United States, since it is inherent in its constitution. Rousseau was no constitutionalist, but a democratic absolutist; whatever the general will decides, is right, because rationality is comprehensible only in terms of the general will. But this absolutist reason of state leads to Kant's constitutional form; here the arbitrary will of the collective is once more provided with a rational underpinning in the doctrine of the categorical imperative. This categorical imperative wills the security and survival of the constitutional order; but since the maintenance of law is an essential pre-condition of the constitutional order itself, the constitutional reason of state wills the scrupulous enforcement of legal rules. However, there remains the external threat and the consequent danger for the maintenance of the constitutional order, as long as no universal constitutional order has been instituted. As a result, the categorical imperative also wills the establishment of such an universal order under law: the achievement of this order is the true constitutional reason of state: to supersede the state by a world constitutionally organized.

The pagan, secular, Machiavellian strand and the Christian and moralist strand are combined into the Hegelian synthesis which interprets only that part of the political organization as "state" in the true sense which is the embodiment of the ethos of a people, which means that the requirements of security and survival of such a state become inherently and necessarily rational. The actual state most nearly approaching this ideal state is the monarchical constitutional state, in Hegel's view, because it is the most advanced form of state which the historical evolution has brought about. History embodies the forward march of the world spirit, and the state is its most potent instrumentality. Hence reason of state, and more especially constitutional reason of state are given limitless scope to achieve the security and survival of this historically, and hence spiritually sanctified order. War, far from being a hindrance to this achievement, as in Kant, actually turns out to be a necessary tool in the hands of the rulers within a constitutional order, as of all other historical orders. For a free world, faced by the totalitarian challenge, Hegel provides the most radical doctrine of constitutional reason of state. The world spirit who wishes constitutionalism to triumph, because it is the most advanced embodiment of freedom, would sanction any measures required for its victory.

From Machiavelli to Hegel, writers on politics who were tough-minded enough to appreciate the problems of survival, would readily admit that there is no such thing as absolute security. Yet, much contemporary thinking proceeds on this assumption, and an attentive reader of the hearings of Congressional bodies[3] will readily discover the extent to which this notion is at work. Against such views, we insist that true security can only be achieved as individual and collective move forward, meeting the challenges as they arise. That is to say, security is not an absolute antithesis to risk, but can only be realized through risk-taking. Yet a risk to provide a chance for security and survival, must be what the military call a "calculated risk." That is to say, it must be related to a weighing of alternatives, alternative roads toward a reasonably well-defined goal. Now, in a sense survival is such a goal, primitive to be sure, but also very basic. Still, survival of a constitutional order involves more than mere self-preservation, because of the rational, the spiritual content of this kind of order. If the maintenance of constitutional freedom, of civil liberties or

[3] Cf. e.g. the hearings entitled *Commission on Government Security,* held before a Subcommittee on Reorganization of the Committee on Government Operations, U.S. Senate, 84. Congress, March 9-15, 1955.

basic rights[4] is implicit in the goal of survival, then their suppression becomes paradoxical. We cannot retreat with Hegel into the cloudy and mystical realm of the world spirit and its undisclosed workings. A rational solution of this problem in constitutional terms imposes itself as the very essence of constitutional reason of state. It is going to involve the taking of calculated risks; but without risks, there can be no security; hence the paradoxical confusion of the term "security risk" to designate a person not wanted in a threatened constitutional order, when it should designate a person who is wanted for the security of the constitutional order, although or indeed *because* he is a risk, but a risk worth taking.

Within the framework of this range of ideas, certain approaches to the problem in the constitutional and administrative practice of our times might be more fruitfully examined. The particular way in which England and France, Italy and Germany, as well as some of the smaller nations of Europe have sought to deal with the problem of security, might be profitably juxtaposed to present trends in the United States. It is my belief that something more promising can reasonably be advocated as a viable solution to the problems of security and survival than has so far been embodied into the law of any of the existing constitutional systems of which the free world is composed. A more detailed analysis I hope to give on another occasion. Right here it might be interesting, though, to cast a fleeting glance at the diversity of solutions attempted in several present-day constitutional systems. For there is extraordinary variety, and the reasons for this variety are not, at the moment, very clear unless it be the difficulty and com-

[4] On the evolution of the American constitutional semantics from rights to liberties to freedoms, I gave some brief hints in "Rights, Liberties, Freedoms" in *University of Pennsylvania Law Review*, vol. 91 (1942), p. 312ff.

plexity of the issues involved. Whether any of these solutions really are viable, only experience can tell. A theoretical analysis certainly would leave one very much in doubt. For until now, those constitutional systems which survived, did so not because they had solved the problem of internal security, but because the problem never became sufficiently serious in the liberal age to threaten the existence of these states. Others which perished, notably the constitutions of Italy (1926), Germany (1933) and Czechoslovakia (1948) had not made what one could describe as adequate efforts even at solving the problem. The endlessly debated German *Republikschutzgesetz*[5] certainly cannot be considered adequate in any sense. It is these experiences which have, as a matter of fact, lent poignancy to the search for an answer in our day. The catastrophies of Italy, Germany and Czechoslovakia continually stir the imagination to seek a more effective solution to the problem.

There are today roughly four major modes of approaching the issue of constitutional defense, i.e., of internal constitutional reason of state. The first approach to the problem is to outlaw, by legislation, a party or organization which is engaged in efforts to undermine or destroy the constitutional order and to establish a different and non-constitutional one. This legislative method of solving the problem is found in the United States and Switzerland, with the American legislature slightly restrained by the judicial power of review. The second approach also provides for outlawry of the subversive group or organization, but by way of a judicial decision, made upon request of the executive; such decision may make the organization illegal (Art. 21) or it may deprive the members of the organization in question

---

[5] March 25, 1930. See for this G. Auschütz, *Die Verfassung des Deutschen Reiches* (14 ed., 1932) p. 41ff, and Alexandre Graf Dohna, "Die Staatlichen Symbole und der Schultz der Republik," in *Handbuch des Deutschen Staatsrechts, I,* pp. 200ff (1930).

of certain basic rights, specifically mentioned in the constitution (Art. 18). This is the method employed in the German
Federal Republic. The third approach is through the elimination of presumed subversives from defined positions in
the administrative services, both private and public, either
by administrative regulation or by legislation. This administrative method of dealing with the problem is found in France
and in Italy, but also to a considerable extent in the United
States. Characteristically, the administrative measures are restrained, but at the same time also sanctioned, by an administrative court, such as the *Conseil d'Etat,* or by an administrative commission, such as the president's loyalty board. The
fourth mode is to develop detailed legislation for eliminating
the characteristic practices of such a subversive or totalitarian
group or organization, rather than outlawing the group itself.
This method is illustrated by Britain's Public Order Act of
1936; it is also found in many states of the U.S. There is at
present a wholesome tendency to develop this approach elsewhere, through suitable revisions of the penal law, e.g., in
France and the German Federal Republic.

All these methods possess a certain value, and each one has
given some results. They are to some extent shaped by the
particular constitutional and political traditions of the country.
For example, the *Conseil d'Etat* in France enjoys fairly universal confidence, and its decisions are generally accepted as
fair, while in the United States the same may be said of the
Supreme Court. But basically, the problem remains unresolved. Everyone of the procedures adopted has already
aroused considerable apprehension and controversy and will
no doubt continue to do so. The basic issue which remains unresolved is this: when will anyone of these methods actually
result in undermining the faith in the constitutional order itself,
to the extent that it disintegrates the will to maintain such a

constitutional order? And faith apart, at what point does the application of such procedures destroy the order itself? How long are "basic" rights "basic," when they can be withheld from large groups of citizens? At what point are "indestructible" rights "destroyed" under such circumstances? The enemies of the constitutional order, Communists and Fascists alike, are known to be fully aware of the corroding effect of their tactics. Yet, is not the survival of the constitutional order itself at stake? Can faith be maintained in an order which has lost its inner meaning and vitality? These are the questions which are on the mind of all those who seriously consider these issues.

I personally lean toward the British approach. It seems to me that an effort to eliminate the particular acts of groups or of a party and of the persons composing them which violate the constitutional order as such, which jeopardize the liberties of other citizens and which seriously impede the functioning of the legal order as a whole, is probably the most reasonable and the most efficient mode of procedure. For such an effort leaves intact the fundamental beliefs in law and liberty. It does in fact absorb "constitutional reason of state" into the "criminal law." But this highly pragmatic, empirical approach calls for a principle in terms of which it is developed. It is the principle of calculated security risk which recognizes that we are here confronted with a conflict of values, that liberty and security are both at stake.

What follows from all this thought on reason of state which we have presented and analyzed? Leaving aside external security, what are we to think of these several programs in light of the classical thought on the subject? First of all, it seems clear that any security program should not be left to ordinary legislation, let alone to administrative ordinance and discretion. It must be anchored in the basic law, in the constitution itself. There should be clear and adequate provision for constitutionally safeguarded emergency powers. These powers should be exercised not by those who proclaim the emergency, but by others, duly designated in the basic law, the legislative ones by an elected body different from the ordinary legislature, but not a constitutional court, the administrative (executive) ones by an high official or board different from the chief executive. Whatever action is taken, whether executive or legislative, should be taken in terms of specific violations of previously established law, and not by way of outlawry of organizations or opinions. It should, in other words, define, like the British Public Order Act of 1936, the acts which subversive individuals and groups are forbidden to commit, such as delivering classified information to foreigners, or wearing uniforms and intimidating fellow citizens. Many of these acts are, as a matter of fact, already designated as criminal; note especially the category of treason in existing penal law. But under no circumstances should such persons be deprived of their constitutional rights, as such, and attempts to penalize them for seeking the protection of these rights should themselves be strictly prohibited.[6] If a particular right, such as the Fifth Amendment of the American Constitution is believed to be badly stated or outmoded, a suitable amendment of the constitutional provision should be undertaken. From this viewpoint, such enactments as the Internal Security Act of 1950 appear to be not so much unconstitutional in terms of the existing constitution, as contrary to the spirit and detrimental to the security and survival of constitutionalism as such.

I have no illusion that this or any other constitutional democracy will in fact be adopting such a comprehensive program of defending itself against those who would subvert it.

[6] The objections recently raised against the Fifth Amendment in the United States in this connection are very subversive, and should be stopped; cf. Erwin N. Griswold, *The Fifth Amendment Today* (1955).

Any constitutionalism may well be able to squeeze by with the inadequate safeguards that it in fact possesses. To my way of thinking such plans are formulated by the theorist to serve as guideposts to those who are perplexed by the issue. A rational conduct of politics is forever the true object of constitutionalism; even its partial realization is likely to be aided by delineating the most perfect form that the rational mind can devise. Constitutional reason of state is, I hope to have shown, in the last analysis a matter of ever more effectively ordering a "government of laws." Three hundred years ago, in the great English revolution fought and won for the idea of constitutional liberty, the man who perhaps felt more deeply than any other before or since the paradox, the dialectic which the security and survival of such an order posits, Oliver Cromwell, had despaired of getting his countrymen to adopt such a constitutional order of their own free will. It was the year of Harrington's *Oceana* which, though it was dedicated to him, the Lord Protector would not accept. Perhaps he sensed its pagan quality. But there is something which Oliver Cromwell knew, which he had told his several parliaments and which Harrington appreciated, and it was this: "In every government, there must be somewhat fundamental, somewhat like a *Magna Charta,* that should be standing and be unalterable. . . ." And he knew also, as Spinoza and Kant knew that among these fundamentals, the most fundamental of all is the right of a man to his conviction, his belief, his faith. For here is the hard core of man's dignity. To make his innermost self secure is more vital to the security and survival of a constitutional order than any boundary or any secret. It is the very core of constitutional reason of state. It is the reason why a constitutional state is founded and is maintained.[7]

[7] Two closely related issues are dealt with in my paper "Authority, reason and discretion" in *Authority,* vol. I. of *Nomos*—Yearbook of the American Society of Political and Legal Philosophy (1957).

APPENDIX

Review of Friedrich Meinecke's
Die Idee der Staatsräson in der Neueren Geschichte[1]

THIS BOOK IS WITHOUT DOUBT one of the most important recent contributions to the history of political ideas. It is at the
same time highly suggestive for political theory as such.
Friedrich Meinecke is unrivalled in his ability to unravel the
complexly interwoven transfiguration of a general idea. The
eternal object which such an idea represents becomes intelli-
gible through his masterful exposition of the kaleidoscopic
multiplicity of individual formulations which its various aspects have found. His powerful historical imagination renders
his study of ideas unusually vivid, for he brings to them the sure
touch of the historical scholar who is fully aware of the atmos-
phere or climate of each successive age. Whether or not you
agree with the particular positions taken by the author, you
will always come away with a richer and more subtle point of
view. All this could be, and has often been, said regarding
his epochal *Weltbürgertum und Nationalstaat*. It is equally
true of this more recent study. And in view of the fundamental

[1] (München und Berlin: Druck und Verlag von R. Oldenbourg. 1925.
Pp. 546.)

Reprinted from the *American Political Science Review,* Vol. XXV,
1931, pp. 1064-69, and slightly altered for the purposes of this book.

importance for political science of the notion of a "reason of state" or, more broadly put, of a specifically political type of rationality, you will find yourself reading the various chapters over and over again in an effort to realize all the implications. In this review we wish to concentrate upon a critical evaluation of Meinecke's interpretation of this eternal object of political speculation.

The peculiar excellences of Professor Meinecke's work have tended to prevent a critical evaluation of its fundamental tenets. Its pyschological subtlety, its weighing of antithetical and contradictory opinions, and particularly the refusal to define, or at least to circumscribe, the central concept at the outset intensify the difficulties of the critic. Yet this task seems rather essential and is suggested by some general lines which the book suggests.

The reason of state *(ratio status, raison d'état, ragion di stato, Staatsräson)* was one of the outstanding catchwords of the later sixteenth and early seventeenth centuries. Under the impact of Machiavelli's passionately detached analysis of the conditions of political action, speculation everywhere in Europe turned upon this fundamental problem of the relation of politics to the other realms of human endeavor. The idea of such a separate reason of state is at bottom neither more nor less than the assertion of the state, or organized political community, as the highest of all values.

That certainly was the view of Machiavelli. His thought is, however, complicated by the concept of a *virtù* which, according to Meinecke, is in turn in Machiavelli's opinion the self-evident purpose of the state (p. 43). This heathen concept of *virtù* deserves for this discussion to be made more specific by a few quotations, particularly since it is practically unknown in English (Cf. R. N. Carew in *Hibbert Journal,* October, 1928). "It is an exceedingly rich concept, . . . with a peculiar and individual note. It might include moral qualities, but primarily it is to designate something dynamical, something put by nature into man, heroism and the strength to accomplish great political and military deeds, but particularly to found and maintain flourishing states" (pp. 39-40). "It suggests the emotional and spiritual strength of natural man who through *grandezza dell 'animo* and *fortezza del corpore* grows to be a hero. This *virtù* is either genuine, in which case it produces that rare specimen we call a statesman, or it is derived, and then it produces good citizens. But *virtù* is by no means unregulated force of nature, it is force transformed into rational and purposive conduct, *virtù ordinata.* Associated with this concept of *virtù* are the concepts of *fortuna* and of *necessità.* It is the task of *virtù* to limit the influence of *fortuna.* In this struggle it is permissible to seize upon any promising weapons" (p. 46). "*Necessità* represents another aspect of the set of forces which we should today call the realm of causal determinations. If *virtù* is the living strength of man which creates commonwealths and gives them life and meaning, *necessità* is the causal, coercive force, the means to shape the inert mass into the form desired by *virtù*" (p. 47). Machiavelli's doctrine of *virtù* undertakes to rationalize the passion of some great men to create a community in their own image by the one grand simplification that this is the most important creative effort. Like the ancients, Machiavelli asserts that upon its success depend all other creative efforts as their *conditio sine qua non.* He thus eliminates all possibilities of the conflict of values.

But this doctrine of *virtù* was not understood by his later admirers and detractors. It was a child of the Renaissance, and it disappeared with it (p. 56). The calculating technical attitude toward political problems which this doctrine implies is all that remains under the misleading slogan of "Machiavellism." The idea of the reason of state is its central tenet. Meinecke sets himself the task of discussing the spiritual struggle over this "Machiavellism" in terms of the idea of the reason of state (p. 57), rather than venturing upon a critical study of the literary controversies over Machiavelli *in extenso* (p. 61)—a job which had been done before him by Christ, Mohl, Villari, and Burd.

We have to look now for Meinecke's opinion as to what is to be understood by this concept. Although he tells us that "the rich content of the idea of reason of state cannot be enclosed within the narrow limits of a definition" (p. 251), he often indicates what he wishes to have us understand by reason of state. It is the principle of political action, the law of motion of the state. It tells the statesman what he must do in order to maintain and strengthen the commonwealth, because the state is an organic formation whose full strength is maintained only if it can somehow continue to grow. Reason of state indicates the ways and means of this growth. These formulations as a starting point are a bit vague. Surely if reason of state includes everything that the statesman must do under any circumstances, it lacks all specific significance. If, on the other hand, it embraces certain general rules, as the first sentence suggests—when Meinecke speaks of the law of motion of the state—it would perhaps be better to speak of rules which "usually" work, for the notion that unalterable laws rule throughout the universe is now commonly doubted. In other words, in this latter meaning, reason of state is simply the particular illusion applied to the facts of politics corresponding to similar notions applied to other facts—all presupposing an order of nature as a matter of course.

By operating with a vague concept, Meinecke is enabled to

bring a vast network of heterogeneous ideas into the discussion, but this discussion for the same reason lacks structural clarity. Its effervescent wealth of interrelated ideas receives its order from the sequence of authors whom the discussion takes up in turn. This means that the book as a whole tends to become a series of essays on these individual authors, held together rather loosely, not by any definite *idea* of the reason of state, but rather by the *word*. The various chapters deal particularly with Machiavelli, Gentillet, Bodin, Botero, Boccalini, Campanella, Naudé, Grotius, Hobbes, Spinoza, Pufendorf, Courtilz de Sandras, Rousset, Frederick the Great, Hegel, Fichte, Ranke, and Treitschke. There is also a chapter each on the spread of the doctrine of reason of state in Italy and Germany in the seventeenth century, and on the doctrine of state interest in France in the time of Richelieu.

In the opinion of the reviewer, this selection is not entirely immune from criticism. For example, it is not apparent why so shallow a writer as Gentillet should have been selected as the only Calvinist. The reason for Meinecke's choice must probably be looked for in a distinction which he attempts to draw between the history of ideas and the history of political theories. "To write the history of the idea of the reason of state means to investigate how reason of state has been grasped and explained by human thought during the passage of time. Formerly, one accorded this task to the history of political theories. The latter is usually treated as a sequence of dogmas, loosely connected with general history. Such shallow treatment cannot satisfy us today. The history of ideas should be treated as an essential part of general history . . ." (p. 25). Nobody will quarrel with these propositions. It is certainly true that "only by being grasped in the form of a principle do the tendencies of an historical epoch acquire their full impetus and rise to what one may call an idea" (p. 49). But the crucial problem remains: Which formulations of such a general idea shall we select from among the many available ones? Shall we emphasize those which contemporaries read most widely, or those which fit into a pattern of truth that we are willing to defend on general grounds regarding both their adequacy and consistency? Yet, Meinecke's critical attitude toward what he calls the history of political theories arises from a notable shortcoming of a great deal of political theory, so-called. This difficulty is rooted in the constant confusion of political and juristic concepts, a confusion which is bred by the desire of political pamphleteers to obscure the essential logical distinction between categories of existence and categories of essence, between what is and what ought to be.

The absence of a clearly defined concept of the reason of state does not mean that Meinecke's discussions lack all inner direction. As a matter of fact, Meinecke even speaks of a progress and development in the doctrine. The early doctrine was abstract, rationalistic, generalizing, and mechanistic. It presupposed that human nature was more or less alike in all times and places. The newer doctrine considers the individuality of each state. For Meinecke, the turning point is to be found in the philosophy of the German idealists, particularly Hegel (p. 434 and elsewhere). They expounded, as everybody knows, the identity of nature and reason, of politics and ethics. In order to be able to assert that the existing state is the reasonable (i.e. good) state, Hegel was obliged to deprive reason of its static character, to rob its objects of their eternal validity. Meinecke rightly emphasizes the dominating influence which this variety of anthropocentric monism had in Germany during the nineteenth century. The effect of this doctrine was to palliate *Machtpolitik* by "idealizing" it (p. 533). Thus, idealism became the entering wedge for a coarsely naturalistic and biological *Gewaltethik*. Meinecke minces no words in pointing out that such "idealism" is little better than the Western European "moralism" whose high-flown principles end in lamentations, hypocrisy, or cant.

Meinecke wishes to reject them both. After rejecting the notions developed by German idealism, he propounds a new dualism which reminds one in several respects of American humanism. The doctrine of a distinct political morality he proclaims erroneous. We are here confronted with what is simply a specific instance of a much more general phenomenon, the conflict of individual and universal morality (p. 533). "For every human being, the general, pure, and severe ideal is confronted in each of his actions with his completely individual world which is compounded of natural and spiritual elements. All kinds of conflicts result. . . . The maintenance of his own individuality is certainly a moral right and a moral obligation, whenever it serves to maintain the moral element of this individuality. But if this self-assertion takes place at the expense of the universal moral command, it involves tragic guilt" (p. 534). Applying these general considerations to the political realm, Meinecke insists that the moral code does not lose its validity by coming into conflict with the necessities of political survival, and that he who makes himself the instrument of these necessities must nevertheless accept the odium which attaches to the man who violates the moral code. Unfortunately, the moral code is itself a rather problematical concept. We may readily agree with Meinecke that the moral code, in order to be a moral code, must be considered valid. But the really perplexing question at this point is: "Who decides what is right under certain circumstances?" In other words, the conflict between individual and universal morality, between more or less universal claims of validity, is itself only a limited aspect of the problem of the conflicts of moral and other values, and the concomitant one of the basis of their respective claims to validity. It may be doubted whether we should be satisfied in our efforts to clarify the conflict of fundamental values by taking flight into the aesthetic realm. The word tragedy is at best an expression of the fact that the moral code is itself problematical. It simply indicates the profound shock which the human being suffers when he discovers that conflicts of value do exist, and do require a decision. The fundamental problem of politics is how to organize the community for the purpose of making such final decisions. The idea of the reason of state represents one possible answer. This answer involves necessarily the assertion of a highest value. The highest value it asserts to be the life of the political community to which we belong. If we do not accept this decision, if we wish to assert another highest value, we cannot escape from rejecting the state and the idea of its *ratio*.

Meinecke suggests that the doctrine of *raison d'état* is fundamental for political science (p. 510). In its quest for the concrete "state" it should take account of this "idea." But why limit ourselves to the "state"? Does not the same problem arise wherever the conflict of values takes concrete form? How about the kind of situation epitomized by Dostoyewski in the famous episode of the great inquisitor in the Brothers Karamazov? How about the man who commits a fraud in order to save the business which he knows thousands to depend upon? It seems to the reviewer that the analysis of the real problem of which the historical discussions about the reason of state are only a specific manifestation requires much more exact and searching theoretical analysis before the "idea" can be more than a crude measure of the "political" element in men's behavior. The idea of a specific reason of state may be, and in the opinion of the reviewer it is, the starting point for a fundamental category of political science; but it is no more.

It would be difficult to undertake a detailed evaluation of the wealth of material presented in the book. Several chapters, particularly the first devoted to Machiavelli, deserve a review of their own. The abundance of historical insight and the survey of four centuries of political thought will excite the highest admiration. They will induce anyone who is interested in the history of political ideas to reconsider many of the prominent thinkers of the modern period and to see them in a new light.

Index

129